WEST COAST COOKBOOK

BERGRIVIER VISSERSVROUEVERENIGING

edited by INA PAARMAN

introduction by DR ERNEST MESSINA

Preface

In March 2001, on behalf of the Bergrivier Vissersvrouevereniging (Saldanha branch), Dr Neville Sweijd, then Deputy Director of the International Ocean Institute, Southern Africa, at the University of the Western Cape, approached me to join their book project. The temptation was irresistible.

I wholeheartedly endorse the philosophy of the great Italian food writer, Pellgrino Artusi, who said, 'Italy's culinary gold lies in the hands of our mothers and grandmothers.' The same applies to the fisherwomen along our Cape West Coast. They are an exceptional breed of real foodies!

West Coast Cookbook captures the essence of a great South African culinary tradition. My role was to ensure a high professional standard and to assist with recipe selection and testing. It was a most uplifting and gratifying experience. This is a book of simple food, but when prepared with care, using the best fresh ingredients, the food becomes truly exceptional. To appeal to the contemporary cook, the food was garnished in keeping with modern presentation trends.

The proceeds from this project will go towards job and income creation activities and a tertiary educational trust for the 176 families involved. I wish them well and thank the members warmly for their trust in me and for sharing so generously with all of us who love to eat well.

INA PAARMAN, 2003

It was a beautiful autumn afternoon on the West Coast when we conceived this project over coffee, scones, cheese and jam with the special ladies of the Saldanha Branch of the Bergrivier Vissersvrouevereniging. For the International Ocean Institute, Southern Africa (IOI-SA), it was a delight and an honour to assist the Vereniging with the creation of development projects. The goals of the Vereniging are noble and important, as well as an example of what empowerment and corrective action are all about. Saldanha is steeped in an almost secret, but enormously rich, culture and tradition that was marginalized for most of history. As with the sense of smell and memory, food and cultural history are closely linked and thus the idea for this project was such a natural one, that it almost had to happen. The enthusiasm of Ina Paarman was a major boost for us all and we are grateful and very proud of the results. Our personal history in Saldanha and the West Coast, combined with our love for the sea and its fresh bounty, have made this a meaningful endeavour indeed.

IOI-SA is situated within the Department of Biodiversity and Conservation Biology at the University of the Western Cape. Its involvement in sustainable livelihood initiatives resulted in our participation in this project, the fruition of which was possible with the generous assistance of many dedicated people to whom IOI-SA expresses its utmost gratitude.

Good luck and enjoy the food!

NEVILLE SWEIJD AND JOCELYN COLLINS
IOI-SA, 2003

ABBREVIATIONS USED IN RECIPES: c = cup T = tablespoon t = teaspoon

Contents

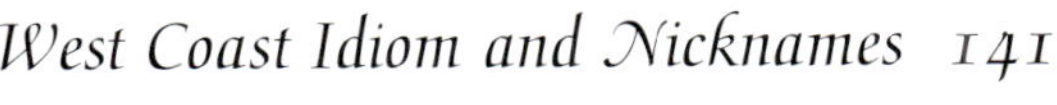

BR41
BR 43
MALMOK
SBH-526

Olifants River
Vredendal
Papendorp
Strandfontein
CEDERBERG
Lambert's Bay
Clanwilliam
Graafwater
Leipoldtville
Elandsbaai
ATLANTIC OCEAN
Redelinghuys
Citrusdal
Dwarskersbos
Aurora
Stompneusbaai
St Helena Bay
Velddrif
Goedverwacht
Paternoster
Piketberg
Vredenburg
Bergrivier
Great Berg River
Saldanha
Hopefield
N
Langebaan
Moorreesburg
Churchhaven
Yzerfontein
Darling
Dassen Island
Malmesbury

A Glimpse into Life in Traditional West Coast Fishing Communities

Late afternoon, and in the background there's the far-off boom of the sea … a group of little boys play, without a care in the world, in the last remaining dusty-white streets of Saldanha. In St Helena Bay, about 40 km away, the scene is much the same. A group of youngsters spin their tops one last time before they are called inside for supper. It's the end of another day. There's not much chance that supper will be seafood. The chances are even slimmer that these young boys will, one day, go to sea as fishermen, like their fathers and grandfathers before them. On the West Coast of the early 21st century, life has changed permanently. 'Even the fish doesn't taste as good,' murmurs Auntie Cathariena Williams, at 82 one of the oldest Saldanha Bay inhabitants.

In the middle of the 20th century, schools were few and far between on the West Coast. Boys were destined for the life of a fisherman, and girls spent their adult lives in a fish factory. Today, in the new, democratic South Africa, there are numerous work opportunities; and the city, industry and tertiary institutions in Stellenbosch, Bellville and Cape Town are open to all who want to follow exciting careers. A bright future beckons young people, offering new opportunities, which they can grasp if they wish, as the experiences of their forefathers tell a dramatically different story.

Very little has been written about the traditional fishing communities of the West Coast. Books focus on white families such as the Silvermans, Stephan brothers and Eigelaars. A few theses have been written about the crayfish industry, St Helena Bay and one or two other subjects, but 'our history has never been written down,' say the women. 'And so many of the old people have died. They could have told so much about the old days … I can't remember too clearly any more either – no, I don't want to be in a book, and please don't put me on the TV,' is the bashful answer from a number of elderly women. Others talk easily about their life beside and on the

Aunt Suzie Julius (85) – regarded as a pioneer – became a supervisor in a fish factory at a time when such a position was unheard of for women, particularly from disadvantaged communities. She held this position for over 30 years.

sea. A few visits later, they realize that you are really interested in their story and the ice is broken. Pen and paper are drawn near, the video camera rolls and the rich story of the traditional West Coast people unfolds from their own remembrances – out of the mouths of the people themselves, with their unique West Coast accent and idiom.

LONG-GONE, FORGOTTEN PAST

Even though the world is going through a modern, highly technological period, thinking about the sea and fishermen conjures up nostalgic, even mystical, images. As in other parts of the world, the sea provided West Coast people with an income, recreation and their daily bread. But with it came pain and heartbreak, when the sea claimed its 'annual harvest' of drowned fishermen. The entire existence of West Coast people was irrevocably bound up with this powerful mass of water, interwoven with grief, joy and hope.

Long before the earliest European explorers braved the sea and the weather to explore the African coast, the Cape's earliest indigenous people, the Khoikhoi, lived off the sea. Tribes who inhabited the West Coast area were the ChariGuriQuas, the CochoQuas and the GrigriQuas in the Langebaan, Saldanha and St Helena Bay areas, respectively. It's not clear what the indigenous Khoikhoi called the West Coast, but early European settlers called the CochoQuas the Saldanhars.

Recently, one of the oldest woman's footprints in Africa was discovered at Kraalbaai in the vicinity of Langebaan. Archaeologists, in particular, were ecstatic at this sandstone find, now called Eva's footprint, which dates back 117 000 years. Archaeological and written sources, as well as the cultural heritage, attest to a significant presence of Khoikhoi tribes. Over a period of hundreds of years, early Portuguese, Dutch, English, Scottish, German and French seafarers and immigrants, and even some from as far away as Iceland, made a landfall on the West Coast. Contact with the local Khoikhoi inhabitants emphasized physical, moral, cultural and language differences. Control of, and access to, the riches of the sea led to conflict between the Khoikhoi and the European explorers. It is still, today, a sensitive subject.

Vasco da Gama, the Portuguese seafarer, made contact with the GrigriQuas when he landed at

Evidence of Khoikhoi settlements located along the Cape coast may be seen in this etching by A. Bogaert entitled 'Historische Reizen' (1711) showing Table Mountain and Bay c.1706.

St Helena Bay in 1497. In the late 15th century, contact between the European civilized world and the natural existence of the indigenous inhabitants of the south-western tip of Africa led to a series of misunderstandings and conflict. One cause of these conflicts was, it appears, the use of natural resources such as water. Until fairly recently, one of the historical water wells in St Helena Bay was called 'Da Gama's well'. Naturally, the Khoikhoi inhabitants used the well as an important life-giving resource long before Da Gama's arrival. Some of these wells, covered by wind and sand over the years, were pointed out to us by 'Oom' April Snyders, an 80-year-old inhabitant of Steenberg's Cove, in the course of an inspection tour of the Britannia Bay area. He even mentioned ostrich eggs and potsherds he discovered, as a child, in the area near the house where he was born. 'Oom' April, a real character and one of the legends of the West Coast, is regularly visited by researchers from far and wide to discuss West Coast history. 'I've wanted to speak on video for a long time,' he says proudly, with laughing eyes, 'because once I have died, the history will be lost.' With our visit, his wish has been fulfilled and his memories immortalized.

'Oom' April Snyders – a respected church official, a builder of fishing boats and a celebrated authority on the history of the people of the Cape West Coast.

Signs of European influences on West Coast culture are in strong evidence. The names of towns, religious practices, ownership, and social and spatial groupings attest to decades of divisive displacement. Saldanha, named after Antonio de Saldanha, a Portuguese seafarer who never saw the town, is by far the best-known West Coast town. From Yzerfontein in the south to Viswater further north, on the mouth of the Olifants River, coastal and inland towns like Langebaan, Vredenburg, Paternoster, St Helena Bay, Velddrif, Laaiplek, Lambert's Bay, Doringbaai, Hopefield and Goedverwacht all bear names that are European in origin. West Coast names mirror the eras of various European influences – Portuguese, French, Italians, Dutch and English. Name changes also took place over the years. The area known as Hoedjiesbaai today was first named Pottersbaai, after a Dutch surveyor, later Houtjesbaai and then Hoedjesbaai. Over the centuries, the sea, the unique flora and the physical environment were a great attraction to travellers, adventurers and settlers. In the process of cultural contact, indigenous people were systematically marginalized, and isolated from their cultural heritage and their land.

The descendants of the West Coast Khoikhoi know little about this history, and there is no enthusiasm for their cultural heritage. Almost without exception, they know nothing about Gonema, the Khoikhoi leader who vigorously resisted European invasion of his area. His name appears to have survived only as Gonemanskraal, a holiday home development at Jacobsbaai. As with many other Khoikhoi descendants, the European line in their genealogical tree is emphasized.

ERA OF COMMERCIALIZATION

In earliest times, people lived off the sea without the restriction of any regulations, except those imposed by Nature herself. Before 1874, fishermen viewed the sea simply as a natural resource. Fish were plentiful. Access to the resource was unlimited and offered great security. Sharing and community support were

Saldanha
SOUTH AFRICAN SCALE
CO. PTY LTD.

characteristic, especially among families who did not have a lot. Fish and crayfish were intended to satisfy daily needs – not to build up wealth.

People like the Scot Alexander MacLachlan and his brother, James, were pioneers in the fishing industry. The first MacLachlans arrived in South Africa in 1813, when their ship was stranded at Stompneusbaai during a storm. Other members of the family followed in 1816 and 1822. James was the skipper of the *Barbara* and the *Alibama*, which started trade with Mauritius. Dried snoek was exchanged for wheat and other valuable goods and brought back to Stompneusbaai.

Commercialization started to gain a foothold in 1874, with the processing of crayfish, driven by a demand that came primarily from Europe. The capital requirements for this industry were huge; far beyond the means of traditional fishermen. Early in the 20th century the crayfish industry was formally established by the Silverman family and the Stephan brothers in Saldanha (1905), St Helena Bay (1915) and Paternoster (1917). Today, crayfish is a sought-after delicacy.

Over time, the entire fishing industry became regulated, and was divided into three main sectors, namely the trawling, pelagic and crayfish industries. Successive governments, from the colonial period up to just before South Africa's first democratic dispensation, excluded West Coast people from the political and economic mainstream. In spite of the Diemont Commission, appointed in 1986 to investigate the industry and make recommendations for its control, the control measures put in place since 1989 took the form of quotas, minimum sizes, and the limiting of areas and seasons for fishing. In this way, the traditional fisherman's access to the resource was limited and led to greater poverty. Crayfish quotas were mainly granted to whites – in 1992, 91% of the 2 million-kilogram harvest was allocated to them. Such imbalances led to previously unknown bitterness among traditional fishermen.

A fish factory complex in Saldanha during the fishing season – fishing vessels line up to offload their catch.

Together with low earnings, a great restriction was placed on what people could eat, their lifestyle and the education they could offer their children.

Under the presidencies of Mandela and Mbeki, the government introduced further restrictions, through regulations and legislation, to obtain better control over fish resources. Although more traditional fishermen at present hold quotas, legislation has substantially influenced their way of life, and the way the industry is handled remains a thorny question.

Marginalization meant that traditional fishermen were less self-sufficient and less able to provide for themselves. The perception that crayfish, and even fish, is the food of the poor changed gradually. These days, crayfish is so scarce that it is rightly known as 'red gold'. Inadequate attempts were made to redress the situation through the establishment of Drommedaris Fisheries, principally for coloureds, under the banner of the former Coloured Development Corporation. Since the 1990s, limited ownership has been obtained by shareholding in individual boats. Other fishermen, such as Davey Clarke of St Helena Bay, erected the first factory, Laingville Fisheries. The factory is completely controlled and run by traditional fishermen, who have their own boats.

INEVITABLE MODERNIZATION

Modernization affected the lives of all West Coast inhabitants in the various areas. The first person to recognize the need for electrical power was John Loubser, popularly known as 'Oom' John Bril (John Spectacles), the owner of the Union Garage in Vredenburg. In 1927, he requested the town's council to provide power lines and poles. The change to electricity met with resistance, but brought with it far-reaching changes, especially after Eskom took over the provision of electrical power in 1952.

View of the road leading to the wharf where boats were anchored during celebrations of the first Sea Harvest Festival in Saldanha in 1963.

The era before electricity – this woman removes baked bread from a typical outdoor clay oven.

The era of candlelight and lamps was gone forever. Cooking methods, and households, were changed with the introduction of electrical power. The coal range and the outdoor clay oven were gradually replaced by modern equipment, although gas and paraffin were still used by poorer people, because they could not afford electrical appliances.

Large-scale changes were also introduced in the fishing industry. Factories were systematically mechanized and this led to longer working hours and an increase in productivity. Ordinary diesel generators, once used by factories such as Saldanha Bay Canning, Southern Seas and by hotels, now were only used in emergencies. Electrification brought with it permanent social and economic changes.

The decline in fish catches meant that factories had to diversify. The fishing industry became part of the food industry, specialization followed and less fish and seafood were available to simply give away. Every possible link in the food chain was exploited, with pets, especially cats, increasingly becoming an important market for excess fish products.

COURAGEOUS MEN

Unlike today, at that time there were no lessons in survival. Parents, conscious of the dangers of the sea and of drowning, forbade their children to go into too-deep water, with the result that many fishermen could not swim. Many tales are told of men who narrowly escaped death. Fishermen often fell out of the boat, into the water, but were miraculously saved.

Very few children were taught what life at sea encompassed. 'At first, we simply went to sea with the older men, and then we stole with our eyes.' Knowledge of the sea, of common practices and the catching of fish were carried over from father to son and from generation to generation.

Fishermen received very little formal education and their far from perfect schooling prevented many of them from enrolling for any further study courses. For this reason, few progressed to becoming skippers; the formal examination frightened them off. In addition, the majority of fishermen managed to earn enough to survive, but had little money left over to save and to build up capital. Moreover, lack of

Attie van Rooyen and Colin Williams (seated) from St Helena Bay.

The 1946 team of the Primrose Rugby Club, Hopefield – the majority of these players were fishermen.

individuality and a long-term vision meant that most of them were incapable of building up material prosperity. The severity of life at sea, a lack of ambition to rise above their circumstances as well as the drinking habit meant that most fishermen focused on the here and now.

Fishermen's incomes were both uncertain and irregular, because of the nature of earning a living at sea. The strict requirements demanded by banks prevented fishermen from obtaining loans to buy their own boats and equipment. Coupled with this, fishermen had little interest in happenings outside the borders of the West Coast, which made their lives relatively isolated. If there was fish, there was food, and with this they were more or less content. There was little recreation, but those who could, played rugby at weekends during the rugby season. Some West Coast teams, such as the Tigers, Buffaloes, Louwenians and St Helena Bay have rugby traditions that extend over many decades.

STEADFAST WOMEN

Providing food for the household was never really a problem for West Coast parents. For many years, fish was the staple food. But times were hard, because specific fish seasons only lasted for a few months. Of even more importance were the influence and vagaries of the weather. In addition, fish was scarce during the summer months because pelagic fish flourish in cold sea currents. Most fishermen worked ashore during the off season, mainly in construction and as bricklayers. In between, they caught harders (mullet), not only to supplement their income, but also for the sheer enjoyment of it, they confess.

The women ran the households and, for the most part, had to face the same kind of challenges. Hardship and poverty were overcome creatively, and the fishermen's wives played a central role in this struggle for survival. Their image does not comply with the stereotype of the unsophisticated, unrefined fisherman's wife. These women were, and still are, religious, hard-working and honourable in their natural role as steadfast women, mothers and workers.

One of the oldest West Coast inhabitants is Auntie Cathariena Williams, born on 1 August, 1920. She has lived in Saldanha all her life. In spite of her advanced age, her memory is crystal clear. As a young child she, like many other children, was educated at the local primary school. At that time, St Andrews was known as 'die skooltjie by die see' (the little school beside the sea). She left school in 1934 to go to work. Most girls of her age worked either in the local hotel, or in one of the fish factories – at that stage Saldanha Canning or Southern Seas. In addition to school, she had to help with household tasks. Saturday was wash day, and it was the children's job to carry the washing, in baskets, up Hoedjieskop, to one of the town's water wells. The water in the Hoedjieskop well was apparently not too brackish, which is why the washing was done there.

For years, the familiar factory whistle shrilly broke the night-time quiet, acting as an alarm to alert the community when boats, fully laden with fish, came in. Working in the factory was not easy. The women had to work night and day shifts because, quite simply, when the fish came in, it had to be processed as quickly as possible. At that time, fish packers earned a penny for every 24 cans of fish packed. During the fishing season, the women worked for hours, without gloves, to process the fish. The fish bones cut into their hands, but they continued working, bloody hands notwithstanding. Today, many West Coast women have problems resulting from fingers and hands that have been permanently damaged; it's common to find crooked fingers, painful backs and arms, as well as scars from many years of working in unfavourable conditions.

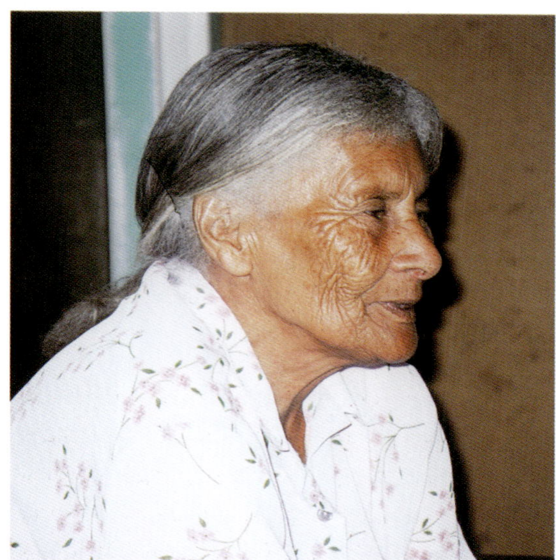

Auntie Cathariena Williams

In the 1960s, fish were plentiful and as many pairs of hands as possible were needed to help in the processing. Fourteen days after the birth of her baby, a new mother had to be back at work. Family members brought very small babies to the factories at certain times of the day, as the mothers had to breastfeed their babies during working hours. At three months, the babies started eating more solid foods. Dough was kneaded and baked in the oven until a crust formed. The mother then mixed the soft insides with fish, chewed it finely, and fed it to the baby. Children were, indeed, raised with fish from the sea, and literally fed from their mothers' mouths. 'Many of us lost our jobs when people began to complain about the smell of the fish-meal factories,' says Alice Griffiths. 'So we had to look for something else, or just stay at home. What else could we do?'

An extra income was essential, because the men's working conditions were characterized by uncertainty and a small, irregular income. This income, from catching fish, was mainly used to buy food. Money was also needed for rent, furniture, motor vehicles and clothes. Most fishermen lived in semi-detached houses with limited space and privacy. The quality of life of fishermen and their families was thus never high. Later, some began building their own houses, and this was their greatest expense.

In times when fish were scarce, men worked in Walvis Bay in Namibia and Las Palmas on the Canary Islands, which meant that they were away from home for long periods. There are numerous, highly romanticized representations of fishermen as adventurous, daring, and full of bravado, defying the elements; men who enter unknown waters, pitting boat against wave, to reap the harvest of the sea. Fishermen always return to the sea, answering its call, because, it is said, salt water is in their blood.

Corrugated iron houses in Steenberg's Cove, St Helena Bay. Aunt Tottie Cloete grew up here.

Because their men were away for so long, the women had to face great challenges. Women have stood, tears in their eyes, watching the boats depart, cutting a path through the waves, as sea birds dart around the mast of the boat, sweeping and soaring, searching for fish scraps or entrails. Often, the salty taste of a tear mingled with the sea breeze, blown landward by a light north-westerly.

Still, the women were proud of their brave men, and silently offered prayers to help carry their loved ones safely across the wide sea. Eyes and hearts were brimming with tears, and hope, and an inner conviction that they would see their men return safely to the harbour; a prospect that resounded in their hearts in a song of longing.

And as the boat grew smaller and smaller and finally disappeared over the horizon, being a woman gained another dimension. While the men were away, running the household lay with the women. Men who worked away from home only returned every six months. Sometimes they sent money by post or telegram, but often they brought cash with them, 'gegorrel om die pens' (tied around the stomach). For long periods, women had to support the household with their extra income. Years ago, children picked up bird feathers at Brandewynbaai, which were then used to stuff pillows and mattresses. Sometimes feathers were exchanged for basic groceries. Bedding made from picked-up feathers is still in use.

Great demands were made on women, who had to be strong spiritually, intellectually and emotionally, not least because their husbands sometimes fathered children in far-off places. They stood by their men, through calm waters and the storms of life, and to this generation of women, divorce was largely unknown. 'Gollietjie likes his drink, and when I fell pregnant as a young girl, my teacher did not want me to marry him because he was very mixed-up. But we've been married for 49 years,' says Aunt Baby Coetzee, with great compassion and no bitterness.

STAUNCH BELIEVERS

Religion and the church have played a central role in the lives of West Coast people for decades. Fishermen face the possibility of dying every time they fare out on a voyage, and they are all too aware of this. During storms, they sing well-loved hymns, and they are deeply grateful when they survive. Their belief that God provides their daily bread is unshakable; beautiful altar cloths, embroidered with 'The Lord is my Shepherd', attest to this.

Over the years, the Anglican Church has had a great influence on the West Coast. Fishermen still bear witness to the role of religion in their lives, and how important it is, with the uncertainty of work at sea. The presence of other churches, such as the former Dutch Reformed Mission Church and charismatic churches, only came about much later, when people moved to the West Coast from other areas, especially Namaqualand, where work had become scarce as a result of the closure of the copper mines. This brought with it further division and shared tensions towards the newcomers.

EDUCATION AND SCHOOLING

During the early years, distances and lack of money made it imperative that children leave school early. Distances made further education virtually impossible, and severely limited career opportunities. Sons, and to a lesser extent daughters, were exposed early to the life their fathers and their grandfathers had had to accept in the absence of other opportunities to find work. 'My husband raised his children from the sea,' says Aunt Tos Basson.

The Anglican Church established various church schools on the West Coast. Stephan was one of the pioneers of this development, and a number of primary schools, such as St Andrew's in Saldanha, were started early in the 20th century as a result of trading with the inhabitants of the various towns. Primary schools were also established in other towns, such as Vredenburg, Paternoster, St Helena Bay, Velddrif, Laaiplek, Doringbaai and Lambert's Bay. Where possible, teachers were drawn locally, but frequently they came from Cape Town or Paarl to teach. During the 1950s and 1960s, the closest high school was in Malmesbury, 80 km away. Shortly after the Group Areas Act came into force, little schools were either moved or became state schools. St Andrew's, for example, was moved to White City – ironically, an area for coloured people. 'Everyone, old and young, was sad to think that we had to say goodbye to a well-loved old "Skooltjie op die Strand" (little school on the beach).' After the 1980s, all schools became state schools, and ties with the Anglican Church were broken.

KAP 'N STERN ... GEE BOE-LYN

These conditions still exist in the collective heritage, where decades of oppression have left psychological scars on individuals and on an entire community, and it will take many more years to redress. Change remains a part of all communities, no matter how gradually it occurs. A future free of bitterness is perhaps extremely difficult to attain, but life is a struggle, and fishermen and their women have, up to now, survived. The days of depending solely on experience and intuition are gone. The future is determined by what we do in the present. This realization should, indeed, encourage West Coast people to say: 'Kap 'n stern' (turn the boat). And though they may already have lost, their rally call to one another should now ring out even louder: 'Kom, kêrels, kom; trek tou op, ons gaan huistoe ... gee boe-lyn' (Come on guys, pull in the rope [the anchor rope], we are going home ... we have enough), as enormous, new challenges and opportunities do indeed lie ahead.

Aunt Tos Basson, an inhabitant of Saldanha, worked for Saldanha Bay Canning. Her husband was a fisherman.

Fish Facts

ANGELFISH (POMFERT)
Brownish in colour with a silver belly, ± 70 cm in length. Medium oil content, very good taste. Firm, whitish flesh, but bony – best filleted before cooking.

GALJOEN (BLACK BREAM)
Found only in South African waters. Colour varies from black to silvery according to location, ± 65 cm in length. Firm dark-veined flesh, high in oil content and a strong, distinctive flavour.

HAKE (STOCKFISH)
A relatively large fish, up to 120 cm in length, but averaging 50–75 cm, silvery-grey in colour. Commonly known as stockfish, it's called haddock when smoked. Low in oil content, the flesh is soft, has a light, delicate flavour and flakes easily.

HARDER (MULLET)
Silvery in colour, it grows up to 60 cm in length, but the average catch is much smaller. Firm, bony flesh with a high oil content and a characteristic flavour.

HOTTENTOT (BRONZE BREAM)
A common food fish in the Cape, it is greyish or brownish on the back with a silvery belly and grows to ± 45 cm in length. Large specimens can be quite fat. The soft, moist flesh has a medium oil content and good flavour.

KABELJOU (KOB)
A large fish – up to 80 cm in length, silvery in colour with a bluish iridescence. The medium-firm flesh has a low oil content and delicate but tasty flavour.

KINGKLIP (LING)
Grows to a length of 150 cm, mottled in colour varying from brown to a salmon pink, with characteristic 'whiskers' below the lower jaw. Low in oil content, it is one of the finest eating fish from South African waters – the liver is regarded as a special delicacy. Firm, moist flesh, but can be dry if overcooked.

Ernest Messina is pictured in both of these photographs with his older brother Mitchell, and their father, with steenbras caught in the mouth of the Olifants River at Papendorp in 1966. Nowadays very rare, steenbras of this size (left) have never been caught there since. The residents of Papendorp depend almost entirely on the catch of harders (mullet) for their livelihood.

MAASBANKER (HORSE MACKEREL)
Bluish on top and silvery below, this fish grows to a length of ± 50 cm. It has a high oil content and firm, dark, rich and tasty flesh. Does not freeze well.

MACKEREL (MAKRIEL)
Blue-silver colour with blackish streaks and spots, grows to ± 45 cm. It has a high oil content, firm, darkish flesh and a distinctive taste.

PILCHARD (SARDYN)
Mixed dark and light blue and green colours, with silvery belly and dark spots. Grows up to 30 cm in length, but most commercially caught fish are smaller. It has a high oil content and firm, darkish flesh.

SNOEK (SIERRA)
Bluish-black on top with a silvery belly, it grows to a length of 105 cm. The firm flesh has a high oil content (especially the belly) and a strong taste.

TUNA (TUNNY)
Silver-grey in colour and a streamlined shape, some subspecies can reach 4 m in length. The firm flesh has a high oil content and a rich, 'meaty' taste.

On the West Coast, winter is a time of hardship and scarcity. The weather is often stormy, with rough seas; the boats can't go out and the fish don't run. If the fishermen can't catch fish, they have no income and every cent has to be spent judiciously. However, the promise of a hearty, home-cooked meal at the end of a cold day does much to disperse the gloom of winter.

WINTER COMFORT

Boontjiesop

10–12 SERVINGS

'Boontjiesop' (bean soup), or any other soup for that matter, is a favourite meal, whether the day is hot or cold. Bean soup tastes even better if it's made the day before.

1 packet (500 g) dried sugar beans
1 kg soup bones
1 kg beef (shin or neck)
2 tomatoes
4 large carrots
1 turnip
2 potatoes
1 large onion
4 c (1 litre) cold water
1 can (65 g) tomato paste
5 stalks celery, chopped
±20 c (5 litres) boiling water
salt and pepper to taste

Soak sugar beans overnight. Wash the soup bones and meat and place them in a large saucepan. Cube the tomatoes and add to the meat. Peel and grate the remaining vegetables, except the celery, and add to the meat. Drain and pick over the beans, then add them to the meat, followed by the cold water. Heat to boiling point. Add the tomato paste, chopped celery and a kettleful of boiling water. Each time the mixture comes to the boil, add boiling water as required (3–4 times). After about 3 hours, when the soup is thick and cooked, add salt and pepper. Serve with fresh bread or croûtons.

HINT

When making soup, boil the meat, bones and vegetables in cold water to extract all the meat juices and nutrients.

Pea or lentil soup

6–8 SERVINGS

West Coast people are fond of some meat, which is why 'ertjiesop' (pea soup) and 'lensiesop' (lentil soup) are so popular, especially during the winter months when fish protein is scarce and the boats don't go out.

300 g soup bones or soup meat (preferably beef)
2 large carrots, coarsely grated
2 large onions, coarsely grated
1 turnip, coarsely grated
1 packet (500 g) dried peas or lentils
4 c (1 litre) cold water
±16 c (4 litres) boiling water
1 small bunch soup celery, chopped
salt and pepper to taste

Wash the soup bones or meat and place in a large saucepan. Add all the grated vegetables. Wash and pick over the peas or lentils. Add the peas or lentils and cold water to the saucepan. Bring to boiling point. When the mixture boils, add a kettleful of boiling water and add the celery. Add a kettleful of boiling water each time the soup mixture comes to the boil (2–3 times). When the soup is thick, add salt and pepper. Serve with fresh bread or croûtons.

Boontjiesop

Fish soup in a potjie

8 SERVINGS

A delicious, nutritious soup that goes a long way in times of scarcity.

1 kg whole Hottentot or any line fish
3 carrots
2 turnips
2 tomatoes
2 potatoes
1 onion
4 T (60 ml) butter or margarine
5 whole cloves
10 peppercorns
8 c (2 litres) cold water
5 stalks celery
2 t (10 ml) salt
2 t (10 ml) pepper

Scale, clean and fillet the fish, then cut into pieces. Reserve the head. Wash, peel and grate the vegetables, except the onion and celery. Heat the butter or margarine in a 'potjie' (three-legged pot) or a large saucepan, cube the onion and add it to the saucepan. Braise until transparent and add the whole cloves. Add the grated vegetables, peppercorns and cold water and cook for 15 minutes. Add the fish pieces, the fish head and the celery and allow to simmer slowly for about 10–15 minutes, until the fish is tender. Season with salt and pepper and stir well. Remove the head. Serve with warm homemade bread.

Melksnysels

6–8 SERVINGS

'Melksnysels' (milk noodles) make a tasty winter meal. It's rather like a homemade pasta, cooked in a flavourful, sweetened milk mixture. This is definitely energy food for a hardworking fisherman's family.

1 c (250 ml) cake flour
1 t (5 ml) salt
2 eggs
cold water
8 c (2 litres) milk
125 g butter or margarine
4 pieces stick cinnamon, broken into pieces
1 T (15 ml) dried or 2 T (30 ml) freshly grated orange rind
1 c (250 ml) sugar

Mix the flour and salt together in a mixing bowl and add the eggs. Mix, adding the water gradually, if necessary, to make a soft, elastic dough. Knead very well. Leave the dough to stand for 30 minutes, or longer, under an inverted mixing bowl. Roll the dough out thinly (about 2–3 mm thick) on a floured surface and sprinkle flour over. Roll the dough up like a Swiss roll and slice thinly to create long, thin strips.

Heat the milk, butter or margarine, cinnamon and orange rind together to just before boiling point. Add the dough strips and cook for 25 minutes over moderate heat. When the dough strips rise to the surface, add the sugar and cook until the mixture is thick and creamy.

Fish soup in a potjie

Mussel and haddock soup

6–8 SERVINGS

4 T (60 ml) butter or margarine
2 t (10 ml) oil
2 large onions, finely chopped
3–4 (± 500 g) potatoes, peeled and finely chopped
2 medium carrots, peeled and finely chopped
3 T (45 ml) cake flour
2 c (500 ml) milk
3 c (750 ml) chicken stock (1 cube or 1 T (15 ml) stock powder)
3 T (45 ml) tomato paste
¾ c (190 ml) frozen peas
500 g frozen haddock fillets
2 large bay leaves
1 t (5 ml) salt
1 t (5 ml) pepper
1 kg uncooked mussels in the whole shell, rinsed well
3 T (45 ml) chopped fresh parsley

Heat the butter or margarine and oil in a heavy-based saucepan. Add the onions and fry for 5 minutes. Add the potatoes and carrots and fry for a further 5–7 minutes. Stir in the flour and cook for 1 minute. Stir in the milk, stock and tomato paste and keep stirring until the mixture boils. Add the peas, haddock, bay leaves, salt and pepper. Simmer covered until the potatoes are very soft and the haddock is cooked. Add the mussels and parsley and cook slowly for 5 minutes. Stir lightly and remove the bay leaves. Serve hot with fresh bread.

Pieter Rosant of Goedverwacht, a Moravian mission station. Strong family and trading ties existed between the communities of the West Coast and the Moravian mission stations including Mamre, Goedverwacht and Wuppertal.

If your family likes mussels, this recipe is a winner!

Mussel and haddock soup

HARVEST FROM THE SEA

'When fish were scarce, people lived off the rocks,' says Aunt Tottie Cloete. 'Wednesday was "perdevoetjie" (limpet) day. People simply scraped them off the rocks at Westpoint, St Helena Bay. "Perdevoetjies" were also "Sunday food", when there wasn't money for meat.'

In times past, people were recompensed for their work with a 'Good For' – a shopping voucher, intended for groceries, clothes and household articles only, which could be exchanged at the factory's shop, the only one in the town. It was usually just enough for flour, coffee and sugar, and not enough for meat.

Aunt Tottie's arikreukel salad

arikreukels
potatoes
1 onion, finely chopped
vinegar to taste
salt and pepper to taste

Wash the arikreukels well. Place them in a saucepan of water and boil them for 15 minutes, until cooked. Remove the meat from the shell – a pin or darning needle works well for this. Pinch off the alimentary canal, remove the hard top (called a 'blaartjie' or leaf) and wash again to remove the last grain of sand. Boil a few potatoes until tender, cube them and add to the arikreukels. Add the onion and mix. Season with vinegar, salt and pepper and mix well. Serve with bread.

'Arikreukels' (periwinkles) were picked from the rocks, but they were also sometimes found on the beach. They look like small, black snails. The secret is to wash them thoroughly, otherwise you'll end up with a lot of sand in your mouth.

West Coast mussel paella

6–8 SERVINGS

Vera Bruinders says it's a good idea to steam extra mussels and freeze them. Remove the cooked mussels from the shells and freeze in smallish plastic containers with lids for no longer than a month.

1 kg seafood mix (marinara mix) (optional)
800 g rice
8 c (2 litres) chicken stock
1 kg fresh whole mussels
1 large onion
⅓ c (80 ml) oil
2 sweet peppers (1 red, 1 green), chopped
1 large ripe tomato, skinned and chopped
3 cloves garlic, cut into thin strips
lemon pepper to taste
chopped fresh parsley

If using, thaw the seafood mixture.

Boil the rice in the chicken stock until cooked. Switch off the stove and leave the rice to stand, covered. Remove the beard from the mussels, then wash them well. Stir-fry the onion in oil until golden brown. Add the sweet peppers, tomato and garlic and stir-fry until the vegetables are tender. Add the seafood mix and mussels, and season with lemon pepper. Cover with a lid and shake the pan from time to time. After 5 minutes, the mussels should have opened (discard any that are still closed), and the seafood mix should be cooked. Combine the seafood mixture with the cooked rice and spoon onto a large serving platter. Sprinkle chopped parsley over lavishly and serve with wedges of lemon.

West Coast mussel paella

White mussel pie with potato topping

8–10 SERVINGS

TOPPING
6 large potatoes
2 T (30 ml) butter or margarine
1 t (5 ml) baking powder
½ c (125 ml) milk
1 t (5 ml) grated nutmeg

FILLING
50 white mussels
1 large onion
2 medium potatoes, parboiled and peeled
4 slices bread, soaked in water or milk
6 T (90 ml) chopped fresh parsley
1 T (15 ml) vinegar
2 eggs, beaten
salt and pepper to taste

Preheat the oven to 180 °C. Boil the potatoes for the topping until tender, then drain and mash. Add the butter or margarine, baking powder and milk, and mix until fluffy. For the filling, boil or steam the mussels for about 5 minutes, until just opened (discard any unopened ones). Remove the shell and black lip. Mince the mussels, onion and potatoes finely in a mincer or chop in a food processor. Drain the bread, mash it with a fork and add it to the mussel mixture. Add the parsley, vinegar, eggs and seasoning, mix well and spoon into a greased ovenproof baking dish. Cover the mussel mixture with the topping, make patterns with a fork and sprinkle grated nutmeg over. Bake for 35 minutes, until golden brown. Serve with steamed vegetables.

The Sanders (1956) returning home with a full load.

White mussels are lifted from the beach sand with the feet. Helen Kotze says that, in earlier times, people used the expression 'to jive' out the mussels and this is the origin of the term 'mussel jive'. In the past, collecting mussels was a popular pastime for children. When they had finished collecting mussels, they simply made a fire on the beach. The mussels were cooked in tins the children carried with them, and they tasted marvellous. These days, a permit is required and only 30 black mussels and 50 white mussels per person, per day, may be harvested, so the one-time mussel jive is dying out.

White mussel pie with potato topping

Pan-fried perlemoen

6–8 SERVINGS

'Perlemoen' (abalone) is very sensitive to heat, so follow Leah Smeda's instructions carefully.

1 kg perlemoen, shelled
milk
salt
cake flour
2–3 eggs, beaten
butter or margarine for pan frying

Clean the perlemoen and cut each one into 3–4 thin slices. Beat well with a meat mallet, then soak in milk for 30 minutes. Drain. Salt lightly, roll in flour and dip in beaten egg. Pan-fry on one side in a little butter or margarine, over moderate heat. Turn after 2–3 minutes and fry the other side until golden brown. Do not expose to too much heat, otherwise it will become tough. Serve with tartar sauce and a fresh salad.

Perdevoetjie or perlemoen frikkadels

6 SERVINGS

50 perdevoetjies or
1 kg perlemoen (abalone)
1 onion
1 large potato
1 large carrot
1 c (250 ml) soft breadcrumbs
2 t (10 ml) chopped fresh parsley
salt and pepper to taste
½ t (2,5 ml) grated nutmeg
2 t (10 ml) curry powder
2 eggs
2 t (10 ml) vinegar
2 t (10 ml) sugar
oil for pan frying

Steam the perdevoetjies or perlemoen in a pressure cooker for 5–10 minutes, then remove from the shells. Mince the perdevoetjies or perlemoen alternately with the onion, potato and carrot in a mincer or food processor. Add the breadcrumbs, parsley and seasonings to the minced mixture and mix well. Add the eggs, vinegar and sugar. Mix well. Shape into frikkadels (rissoles) and pan-fry in 2–3 cm deep hot oil. Serve with white rice and vegetables.

HINTS

Drain frikkadels on crumpled brown paper to remove excess fat. After cleaning the perdevoetjies, place them in fresh water and leave overnight, allowing them to swell. In the past, Aunt Tottie simply used the back of a chopper or mallet to bruise the flesh. Usually, she placed them in a piece of fishing net first, so that the meat would not splatter everywhere. If there were not enough perdevoetjies, she simply added a little minced beef.

'Perdevoetjies' (limpets) are available all year round. They cling to the rocks beneath the water, and can be removed with a sharp knife. However a permit is required and only 15 per person, per day, may be harvested.

Paternoster – an integral part of the West Coast fishing community.

Calamari with pasta

6 SERVINGS

This dish freezes well. When needed, simply defrost and reheat until piping hot.

1 kg calamari
2 c (500 ml) water
⅓ c (80 ml) oil
1 onion, chopped
1 sweet pepper, chopped
1 chilli, chopped
1 T (15 ml) garlic paste
2 tomatoes, chopped
1 can (110 g) tomato paste
4 T (60 ml) sugar
1 T (15 ml) salt
1 T (15 ml) pepper
1 packet (500 g) tagliatelle, spaghetti or screw noodles

Cook the calamari for 5 minutes in boiling water and mince it finely in a mincer or food processor. Heat the oil in a saucepan, add the onion, sweet pepper, chilli and garlic paste and braise until the onion mixture is tender. Mix in the tomatoes and tomato paste, and then the sugar. Add the minced calamari, mix well and braise for a few minutes. Taste and season. Place the pasta in boiling salted water, cook until tender and drain. Add the pasta to the braised calamari mixture and mix. Season with salt and pepper. Traditionally served with mashed potatoes or potato salad.

VARIATION

The dish may also be baked in the oven, with grated cheese on top. The calamari may be cubed instead of being minced.

Annie Orlam says the calamari may be prepared a few hours in advance and stored in the refrigerator.

Braised calamari

4 SERVINGS

Hester Basson has an excellent tip for tenderizing calamari, as given in the method below.

5 cloves garlic, finely chopped
1 sweet pepper, chopped
1 chilli, chopped
1 tomato, skinned and chopped
4 T (60 ml) oil
4 whole (± 500 g) calamari tubes
1 c (250 ml) cooked cubed potatoes
½ c (125 ml) frozen peas
½ t (2,5 ml) salt
1 t (5 ml) pepper

Braise the garlic, sweet pepper, chilli and tomato together in the oil. Cut the calamari into rings. Tenderize it by pouring boiling water over and allow to cool slightly for 5–10 minutes. Pour off the water and repeat once. Pour off all the water and add the calamari to the braise. Cook for only 5 minutes. Add the vegetables, then add the salt and pepper. Simmer for a further 3 minutes. Serve with white rice.

Calamari with pasta

Calamari tubes with garlic and peri-peri

6 SERVINGS

If you can't find dried Mozambique chillies, use fresh or dried bird's eye chillies instead for the peri-peri flavour.

1 kg young calamari, cleaned and tubes left whole
2 t (10 ml) crushed garlic
4 T (60 ml) lemon juice
½ cup (125 ml) olive oil
salt and pepper to taste
½ t (2,5 ml) minced dried Mozambique chillies
100 g butter or margarine
4 T (60 ml) chopped fresh parsley

Place the calamari in a glass dish. Mix the garlic, lemon juice, olive oil, salt, pepper and chilli together well. Taste for heat, adding more chilli if desired. Add the mixture to the calamari and make sure that the calamari is covered. Cover with clingfilm and marinate for 1–2 hours in the refrigerator.

Drain the calamari. Pan-fry 10 tubes at a time. Shake the pan often and add a little of the marinade to prevent burning. Fry until nicely browned, then remove from the pan and place on a serving platter. Keep warm. Fry the rest of the calamari, until all the tubes have been cooked. Melt the butter or margarine in the same pan and add the parsley, then pour over the tubes and serve hot with a green salad and crusty bread or savoury rice.

Deep-fried calamari

4–6 SERVINGS

To prevent breadcrumbs from falling off the calamari, Ellen Kotze places the rings – rolled in a crumb and egg mixture – in the refrigerator for 1–2 hours. If you're in a hurry, 20 minutes in the freezer will do the trick.

4 large calamari tubes or 500 g calamari rings
juice of 2 lemons
2 cloves garlic, crushed
1 t (5 ml) salt
2 t (10 ml) pepper
cake flour
1 egg, beaten
2 c (500 ml) fresh or dried breadcrumbs
3 c (750 ml) oil

If using calamari tubes, cut into rings. Mix the lemon juice and garlic, add the calamari and marinate for 1 hour.

Drain the calamari. Season with salt and pepper, roll in flour and dip in beaten egg. Lastly, roll in crumbs and leave in the refrigerator to firm up. Deep-fry a few rings at a time in oil until golden. Serve with savoury rice, tartar sauce and vegetable salad.

VARIATION

Oysters may also be prepared in this way.

INA'S HINT: To tenderize calamari, pour boiling water over the cut calamari rings, leave to stand for 5 minutes then pour off the water. Repeat twice. Then marinate the calamari rings in the marinade mixture as described above.

Deep-fried calamari

Pan-fried calamari

4–6 SERVINGS

2 large or 6–8 small calamari tubes
1 t (5 ml) salt
1 t (5 ml) pepper
½ c (125 ml) cake flour
½ c (125 ml) breadcrumbs
1 t (5 ml) garlic salt
1 egg, beaten
oil for pan-frying

Clean the calamari and cut into smaller portions. Tenderize with boiling water (see Ina's hint, page 38, or below). Bruise the calamari with a meat mallet and season with salt and pepper. Mix the flour, breadcrumbs and garlic salt together. Roll the calamari in the flour mixture and then dip in egg. Pan-fry in hot oil until cooked. Serve immediately with chips.

VARIATION

The flour and egg may be omitted and the calamari simply seasoned with salt and pepper and then pan-fried.

HINT FOR TENDERIZING CALAMARI

Sprinkle a pinch of bicarbonate of soda over cubed calamari to tenderize it. Set aside for a few minutes. Rinse well.

Crayfish frikkadels

4 SERVINGS

The recipe for this delectable 'frikkadel' (rissole) dish comes from Nellie Samsodien.

3 crayfish tails
2 potatoes, peeled and cubed
1 medium onion, chopped
2 eggs, beaten
4 T (60 ml) finely chopped fresh parsley
1 t (5 ml) salt
½ t (2,5 ml) pepper
½ t (2,5 ml) grated nutmeg
3 slices bread, soaked in water
oil for pan-frying

Remove the shell, discard the alimentary canal and cut the crayfish into smaller pieces. Mince the crayfish, potatoes and onion together, or chop the crayfish and grate the vegetables. Add the beaten egg, parsley and seasonings to the crayfish mixture. Mix well. Squeeze the water from the bread, crumble the bread and add to the crayfish mixture. Shape into rissoles. Fry in hot oil until golden brown. Serve as a dainty starter on a bed of soft lettuce, cubed avocado with a small dipping bowl of seafood sauce.

'Will it ever happen, in my lifetime, that I will make 'frikkadels' from crayfish tails? It makes one want to move to the West Coast!' – Ina Paarman

Crayfish released from a suspended basket into cocopans destined for the factory, Lambert's Bay c. 1925.

Oven-baked crayfish tails

6 SERVINGS

6 crayfish tails

CITRUS SAUCE

½ c (125 ml) orange juice
½ c (125 ml) lemon juice
½ t (2,5 ml) mustard powder
½ t (2,5 ml) celery salt
½ t (2,5 ml) onion salt
½ t (2,5 ml) pepper
½ c (125 ml) butter or margarine

GARLIC SAUCE

2 cloves garlic, crushed
6 T (90 ml) chopped fresh parsley
3 T (45 ml) oil
3 T (45 ml) butter or margarine, melted
½ T (7,5 ml) onion salt

For this recipe, you may choose to prepare either of the sauces, or both (reducing the ingredients accordingly) for variety.

Citrus sauce: mix all the ingredients together, except the butter or margarine, and bring to the boil. Gradually add the butter or margarine, beating the sauce constantly as you do so. Garlic sauce: mix all the ingredients together.

To cook the crayfish, preheat the oven to 200 °C. Steam the crayfish in a saucepan for 5 minutes until parboiled. Halve the tails lengthways and remove the alimentary canal. Place the crayfish, flesh side up, on a baking sheet and bake for 15 minutes in the oven. Baste the crayfish from time to time with the sauce of your choice, and cook until done.

VARIATION

To cook the crayfish over the coals, first place it flesh side down on the grid and braai (barbecue) for 5 minutes. Turn, so that the shell is underneath, and braai until cooked, basting with the sauce as you do so.

Crayfish – the West Coast's red gold.

Ellen Kotze says crayfish is done when the meat is white and no longer transparent. Take care not to overcook, otherwise the crayfish will be dry and floury.

Crayfish tails cooked on the coals

Pan-fried crayfish tails

6 SERVINGS

6 crayfish tails
1 t (5 ml) salt
1 t (5 ml) pepper
cake flour
1 egg, beaten
oil for pan-frying

Halve lengthways the uncooked crayfish tails, then remove the shell and alimentary canal. Rinse and season. Roll in flour and then dip in egg. Pan-fry in hot oil until cooked.

VARIATION

Add 1 t (5 ml) curry powder to the flour mixture.

The presence of crayfish cause other fish to leave an area; another reason why certain fish have become so scarce, according to experienced fishermen.

Crayfish salad

8 SERVINGS

6 crayfish tails
1 c (250 ml) mayonnaise
⅖ c (100 ml) tomato sauce
1 t (5 ml) Tabasco sauce
1 T (15 ml) Worcestershire sauce
1 lettuce, washed
1 lemon, cut into wedges

Steam the crayfish tails for 10–12 minutes, until cooked – the shell must be bright red. Remove the shell and alimentary canal and slice the flesh neatly. Add the mayonnaise, tomato sauce, Tabasco sauce and Worcestershire sauce and mix. Chill. Serve on lettuce leaves with lemon wedges.

VARIATION

To make mock crayfish salad, use hake or a mixture of hake and monkfish instead of the crayfish.

HINT

Crayfish retains its flavour best if it is steamed rather than boiled.

Cheryl Stoffberg says that in the days when crayfish were not as scarce and expensive as they are today, and there was no quota system, West Coast people ate this salad often in the summer months. Those were the good old days!

Excellent crayfish starter

6–8 SERVINGS

This recipe is one of Fan Julius' favourites. She says that everyone, without exception, asks for a second helping, or even a third. Fan and her husband Roy have a crayfish quota, but, ironically, she doesn't really eat seafood dishes. Her family and friends, however, are wild about this delicious West Coast 'red gold' recipe, and she often makes it for weddings and parties.

1 kg whole crayfish
¾ c (190 ml) mayonnaise
½ c (125 ml) French salad dressing
1 whole lettuce, shredded
3 tomatoes, chopped
1 avocado, peeled and cubed
1 pineapple, peeled and cubed
½ sweet melon, peeled and cubed
1 green or red pepper, cut into thin strips (optional)
1 onion, finely chopped
a little prepared mustard

Boil the crayfish for about 10 minutes in salted water, until just cooked. Remove the flesh from the shell, discard the alimentary canal and cut the flesh into pieces. Mix the mayonnaise and French salad dressing, add all the other ingredients and mix lightly. Serve in a glass, or on a salad leaf in an oyster shell.

Pilchard salad

4–6 SERVINGS

Daphne Roussouw says this is the perfect salad when fresh fish is not available.

oil for deep-frying
3 slices white bread, cut into 1 cm-cubes
1 lettuce, shredded
½ punnet (125 g) mushrooms, sliced
½ c (125 ml) Cheddar cheese, cubed
1 can (425 g) pilchards in tomato sauce
1 clove garlic, crushed
5 T (75 ml) salad dressing
freshly ground black pepper to taste

Deep-fry the bread cubes until golden brown and spoon out onto kitchen paper. Arrange the lettuce on a salad platter. Arrange the mushrooms, cheese and croûtons on the lettuce. Drain the pilchards and reserve the sauce – do not break the pilchards. Cut the pilchards into strips and arrange on the salad. Mix the sauce from the pilchards, the garlic and salad dressing and set aside. Pour the dressing over just before serving. Season with black pepper and serve with fresh bread.

Snoek pâté

This delectable pâté recipe comes from Bes Summers of Laingville.

500 g cooked snoek
250 g smooth cottage cheese
1 clove garlic, crushed
1 T (15 ml) grated onion
2 T (30 ml) lemon juice
freshly ground black pepper to taste

Remove the fish bones and flake the flesh. Place in a blender and blend with the remaining ingredients, until smooth. Spoon into a serving bowl and chill. Serve with fresh homemade bread or toast.

Smoked snoek tart

6–8 SERVINGS

PASTRY
1¾ c (440 ml) cake flour
a pinch of baking powder
¾ t (4 ml) salt
125 g butter or margarine
1 egg
5 t (25 ml) oil

FILLING
50 g butter or margarine
⅕ c (50 ml) cake flour
¾ t (4 ml) powdered mustard
2 c (500 ml) milk
2 c (500 ml) grated Cheddar cheese
3 eggs, beaten
2 c (500 ml) smoked snoek, flaked
2 t (10 ml) finely chopped fresh parsley

Preheat the oven to 180 °C.

For the pastry case, sift the dry ingredients together. Rub the butter or margarine into the flour with your fingertips, or cut it in, until the mixture resembles breadcrumbs. Beat the egg and oil together, add to the flour mixture and mix to a soft dough with a knife. Press the dough into a greased tart pan.

For the filling, melt the butter or margarine in a saucepan, add the flour and mustard and stir well. Add the milk, increase the heat and stir constantly until the mixture thickens. Remove from the heat and stir in the cheese until most of it has melted. Allow to cool slightly. Stir in the beaten egg – stir constantly. Lastly, add the flaked snoek and parsley, stir well and turn out into the pastry shell. Bake for 30–40 minutes, until set. Serve with a crisp, green salad.

This tasty snoek tart, from Vanessa Summers, will soon become everyone's favourite.

Oven-baked snoek with chutney

6–8 SERVINGS

1 sweet pepper
1 medium onion
1 medium tomato
½ c (125 ml) chutney
2 T (30 ml) French salad dressing
1–2 whole snoek (depending on size of fish), butterflied and rinsed
salt and pepper to taste

Preheat the oven to 200 °C.

Grate the sweet pepper, onion and tomato and place in a mixing bowl. Add the chutney and mix. Add the French dressing and mix. Place the snoek, flesh side up, on a baking sheet, then season. Brush the chutney mixture over and bake for 30 minutes, until just done. Very tasty with freshly baked bread and jam.

Fan Julius is a retired teacher. For the first two years of her married life, she lived with her mother-in-law, 'Aunt' Suzie Julius (85), who was taught to cook by her grandmother. Fan 'stole with her eyes', and later developed her own recipes.

Boiled snoek heads

6 SERVINGS

6 snoek heads
salt and pepper to taste
1 small onion, quartered
3 c (750 ml) water

Cut open the snoek cheeks and remove the gills and cheek flaps. Make an incision in the eyes and remove the eyeballs. Butterfly the heads and season with salt and pepper. Boil the snoek heads, onion and water together for 15 minutes. Serve with vinegar and boiled potatoes.

Eric Wilsnach says that, on the West Coast, boiled snoek heads are regarded as poor man's food – add an onion, salt and a few potatoes and at least there is food on the table.

Snoek head curry

6–8 SERVINGS

6 snoek heads
salt and pepper to taste
1 onion, chopped
2 T (30 ml) oil
1 tomato, chopped
1 sweet pepper, chopped
1 chilli, chopped
4 cloves garlic, crushed
1 t (5 ml) curry powder
1 t (5 ml) turmeric
1 t (5 ml) sugar
1 T (15 ml) vinegar
6 potatoes, peeled and cubed

Cut open the snoek cheeks and remove the gills and cheek flaps. Make an incision in the eyes and remove the eyeballs. Butterfly the heads and season with salt and pepper. Sauté the onion in oil until tender. Add the tomato, sweet pepper, chilli and garlic and braise until tender. Mix the curry powder, turmeric, sugar and vinegar and add to the tomato mixture. Cook until well-blended. Add the potatoes and cook until the potatoes are almost tender. Add the snoek heads and cook until the potatoes are done. Do not cook the heads for too long, otherwise they will disintegrate. Season to taste. Serve with rice and sambal salads.

According to Hester Basson, snoek head curry is commonly known as 'kortkerrie' (quick curry) because it is quick to make and does not call for many ingredients. Traditionally, snoek is either baked or boiled. Grilling snoek, in the oven or out of doors, is a much later development.

Pan-fried snoek heads

8 SERVINGS

Pan-fried snoek heads are one of the West Coast's special delights, simply eaten with one's hands. This is Lientjie Vraagom's special recipe.

8 snoek heads
3 T (45 ml) salt
2–3 t (10–15 ml) pepper
cake flour
oil for pan-frying

Cut open the snoek cheeks and remove the gills and cheek flaps. Make an incision in the eyes and remove the eyeballs. Butterfly the heads and season with salt and pepper. Roll in flour and pan-fry in hot oil until golden brown. Drain on kitchen paper. Serve with bread.

VARIATION

Snoek heads may also be baked in the oven with tomatoes and onions, or braaied over the coals.

Smoorsnoek

12–15 SERVINGS

'Snoekmootjie' (salted snoek portions), used for 'smoorsnoek' (braised snoek), is made during the snoek season, for the months when snoek is scarce. Ellen Fester says it keeps for 6–8 months in a wooden barrel.

2 kg half-dried salted snoek or snoekmootjie (see page 138)
4 large onions, sliced
⅖ c (100 ml) oil
1 sweet pepper, cut into strips
1 kg potatoes, peeled and cubed
black pepper to taste
4 t (20 ml) lemon juice

Soak the fish overnight in water. Drain.

Boil the fish in fresh water until cooked. Drain, but reserve ½ c (125 ml) of the water (stock). Remove the bones and flake the fish. Braise the onions in oil until golden brown, then add the sweet pepper and potatoes and braise until tender. Add some of the reserved fish stock if the mixture is too dry. Add the flaked fish, pepper and lemon juice and cook for 15 minutes. Serve with white rice.

VARIATIONS

Canned snoek may be used instead of snoekmootjie.

For smoorsnoek breyani, mix with white rice and decorate with hard-boiled eggs.

You can also add tomatoes to the smoorsnoek – use 4 skinned tomatoes cut into cubes and add after braising the potatoes.

HINT

For a more intense flavour, use freshly ground black pepper.

Smoorsnoek with cabbage

8 SERVINGS

When Cheryl Stoffberg makes her version of 'smoorsnoek', everyone asks for more!

1,5 kg snoekmootjie (see page 138)
or 1 kg salted snoek
4 large onions, sliced
⅓ c (80 ml) oil
1 sweet pepper, chopped
1 tomato, chopped
1 cabbage, shredded
1 kg potatoes, peeled and cubed
salt to taste
1 T (15 ml) black pepper or to taste

Soak the snoekmootjie overnight in water. Drain.

Boil the fish in fresh water until cooked. Drain, but reserve ½ c (125 ml) of the water. Remove the bones and flake the fish. Braise the onions in oil until golden brown, then add the sweet pepper and tomato. Braise for 5 minutes and add the shredded cabbage. Add a little of the reserved water. Cook until the cabbage is soft, add the potatoes and cook for 15 minutes. Add the flaked fish and cook until the potatoes are tender. Season with salt and pepper and serve with white rice.

HINT

To keep salt dry, line the salt cellar with blotting paper.

Oven-baked hake with cheese

6–8 SERVINGS

Fan Julius is proud of this recipe, which she developed herself.

salt to taste
1,5 kg whole hake
2 onions, finely chopped
3 c (750 ml) milk
4 T (60 ml) cornflour
½ t (2,5 ml) sugar
salt to taste
2 c (500 ml) grated Cheddar cheese
1 T (15 ml) garlic or ordinary butter
1 large tomato, skinned and finely chopped
1 sweet pepper, finely chopped
chopped fresh parsley
pinch of peri-peri or cayenne pepper

Preheat the oven to 180 °C. Salt the fish and cook it, with half the onions, in a little water until just done – allow the onion flavour to permeate the fish. Remove the bones and skin, flake the fish and place it in a greased ovenproof dish. Heat the milk. Meanwhile, mix the cornflour to a paste with a little water or milk. Add sugar and salt, as this mixture should not be too bland. When the milk is almost boiling, add the cornflour paste and stir to make a thick, but liquid, sauce. Add 1 cup of grated cheese to the white sauce, then the butter, and heat until both have melted. Add the tomato, sweet pepper, parsley and leftover onions to the flaked fish and mix with a fork. Mix in the white sauce. Season with salt and peri-peri. Sprinkle remaining cheese over and bake for 30–35 minutes. Serve with rice.

HINTS

A transparent ovenproof dish will allow you to watch that the fish does not dry out as it cooks. The quantity of sauce must be in proportion to that of fish, to prevent a too dry or too moist result.

Oven-baked hake with cheese

Fishermen's stew

6 SERVINGS

This mouthwatering dish, from Cynthia Joshua, can be made in a jiffy.

2 T (30 ml) oil
2 large onions, sliced
1 sweet pepper, chopped
1 t (5 ml) garlic paste
1 c (250 ml) uncooked rice
4–6 large tomatoes, grated
2 t (10 ml) salt
1 t (5 ml) cayenne pepper
3 c (750 ml) chicken stock
sugar (optional)
500 g white fish fillets, cut into portions
250 g frozen peas

Heat the oil in a heavy-based saucepan. Braise the onions, sweet pepper and garlic paste until the onions and pepper are tender. Add the uncooked rice and stir until mixed. Add the tomatoes, salt, cayenne pepper and 2½ cups (625 ml) of the stock, cover and simmer for 30 minutes. Taste and add sugar, if necessary. Add the fish to the rice mixture, then stir in the peas and simmer for 10–15 minutes. Make sure it doesn't cook dry – add some of the remaining stock, if necessary. Serve with fresh bread and a mixed salad of your choice.

INA'S HINT: Halve the unpeeled tomatoes horizontally and grate the cut sides on the coarse side of the grater until only the skin remains. Discard the skin.

Curried tuna

8 SERVINGS

Leah Smeda says tuna is a very dry fish and must be prepared correctly if it is to be tasty.

2 kg tuna
salt and pepper to taste
1 c (250 ml) oil
1 c (250 ml) boiling water

CURRY SAUCE
3–4 large onions, sliced
3 T (45 ml) curry powder
1 t (5 ml) turmeric
2 t (10 ml) fish spice or lemon pepper
2 t (10 ml) fish masala
2 T (30 ml) vinegar
sugar to taste

Preheat the oven to 180 °C.

Remove the skin from the tuna and cut the fish into 5 cm-thick portions. Season the fish with salt and pepper and place it in an ovenproof dish. Mix the oil and boiling water and pour it over the fish portions. Bake the fish for 25–30 minutes, until cooked.

For the curry sauce, cook the onions, curry powder, turmeric, fish spice, fish masala and vinegar together. Add sugar to cut the acidity of the vinegar slightly. Pour the hot curry sauce over the cooked fish. Serve hot with rice, or cold with salad.

HINT

The baked fish, without the curry sauce, keeps well in the refrigerator and can be used, like canned tuna, in salads, fish cakes and so on.

Fishermen's stew

Stuffed harders

2 SERVINGS

Like any other oily fish, 'harders' (mullet) are at their best if they are cooked fresh from the sea. This is classic healthy food, says Johanna Coetzee.

2 harders
2 slices bread, soaked in water
1 egg
1 T (15 ml) oil
1 t (5 ml) lemon pepper
1 t (5 ml) salt
1 t (5 ml) pepper
4 t (20 ml) chopped fresh parsley

Preheat the oven to 200 °C.

Scale the harders thoroughly. Cut the fish along the backbone, remove the bones and entrails, then wash the fish and set it aside. Squeeze the water from the bread and mix it with the remaining ingredients. The mixture must not be either too dry or too moist. Stuff the bread mixture into the fish and close the cavity with needle and thread. Bake for 25 minutes. Serve with brown bread, apricot jam and black coffee.

Pan-fried fish

8–10 SERVINGS

1 fresh snoek or other fish (see Variations), butterflied
coarse salt
pepper
oil for pan-frying
cake flour

Sprinkle the snoek with coarse salt. Set aside for 1 hour, then rinse. Cut the snoek into portions and sprinkle pepper over. Heat the oil in a frying pan until very hot – the base of the pan must be covered with oil. Roll the snoek in flour, reduce the heat slightly and pan-fry on one side until golden. Turn the fish over and fry the other side. The skin must be crisp and crackly. Serve with mashed potatoes or chips and braised tomatoes.

VARIATIONS

Use harders, yellowtail, kabeljou, white stumpnose, hake or Hottentot instead of snoek. The fish may also be dipped in egg and then rolled in flour before frying.

HINT

To freeze snoek, sprinkle coarse salt over fresh snoek and set aside for 30 minutes to 1 hour, then rinse off the salt. Cook the snoek and freeze it. Never freeze unsalted fresh snoek, because it will be pulpy when it is thawed. A smallish snoek, once salted, may be set aside for 20 minutes or less.

On the West Coast, Monday night is usually fish night, and the fish is often pan-fried. According to Nellie Samsodien, the secret to successful frying lies in the heat of the oil.

Pan-fried fish

St Helena Bay fish pie

8 SERVINGS

2 kg white fish fillets
1 large onion, sliced
2 small cloves garlic, crushed
1 large bay leaf
½ t (2,5 ml) dried marjoram
salt and pepper to taste
1 c (250 ml) white wine
6 potatoes, peeled
1 T (15 ml) butter or margarine
1 small can anchovies, drained and the oil reserved
2 egg yolks
milk or cream
6 hardboiled eggs, sliced

Preheat the oven to 200 °C.

Use an ovenproof dish with a tight-fitting lid; it must be just large enough to hold all the fish, without allowing too much space around the fillets. Arrange the fish fillets on a layer of onion slices and crushed garlic, with the bay leaf in the centre. Sprinkle over the marjoram and salt and pepper and add enough wine to almost cover the fish. Cover with the lid and bake for 20–30 minutes, until done but not overcooked.

Meanwhile, boil the potatoes until tender. Drain. Mash with the butter or margarine, oil from the anchovies, egg yolks and enough milk or cream to make a fairly moist mixture that is smooth but not runny. Transfer the cooked fish and onions to a large bowl. Flake the fish (not too finely). Quarter the anchovies and mix, together with 3–4 tablespoons (45–60 ml) of mashed potato, with the fish. Arrange the egg slices on top and cover with the mashed potatoes. Level the surface, then use a fork to create a ridged pattern on top. Bake for 25–30 minutes, until heated through and slightly browned on top.

The Neptune – *William 'Willa' Joshua (father of Poy Joshua) was a skipper of this boat, seen here returning from a successful catch.*

St Helena Bay fish pie

Fish pie

8–10 SERVINGS

A simple dish from Caroline Talmakkies in which fish is cooked in a creamy white sauce.

1,5 kg whole hake or kingklip
½ c (125 ml) oil
3 onions, finely chopped
2 T (30 ml) vinegar
1 t (5 ml) curry powder
1 c (250 ml) cooked, cubed potatoes
2 T (30 ml) butter or margarine
1½ T (22,5 ml) cake flour
1 c (250 ml) milk
½ t (2,5 ml) salt
½ t (2,5 ml) pepper

Preheat the oven to 180 °C.

Cook the fish in a pan of salted water. Remove the skin and bones without breaking the fish unnecessarily, and cut it into smaller pieces. Heat the oil in a saucepan, add the onions and sauté until lightly browned. Remove the saucepan from the stove and stir the vinegar and curry powder into the onions. Add the potatoes and mix lightly. Layer the fish and onion mixture in a large, greased ovenproof dish, ending with onion mixture. Melt the butter or margarine and stir in the cake flour. Add the milk gradually, stirring constantly to prevent lumps from forming. Season with salt and pepper. Boil for a further 5 minutes until the white sauce is thick but still liquid. Pour the sauce over the ingredients in the dish, then bake for about 30 minutes, until golden brown. Serve with rice and vegetables.

Aunt Baby's tomato-fish dish

10–12 SERVINGS

Johanna Coetzee often makes this delectable tomato and fish dish for her family.

6 T (90 ml) oil
2 large onions, sliced into rings
1 kg hake fillets
4–5 tomatoes, skinned and sliced
salt and pepper to taste
4 T (60 ml) chopped fresh parsley
½ c (125 ml) fresh breadcrumbs

Preheat the oven to 160 °C.

Pour 2 T (30 ml) oil into a large ovenproof baking dish. Layer the onion rings, fish and tomatoes in the dish, seasoning each layer with salt and pepper. Repeat the layers, ending with a layer of tomato slices. Drizzle the remaining oil over. Mix the parsley and breadcrumbs and sprinkle over. Bake for 30–40 minutes, until golden brown. Serve with chips and steamed vegetables.

VARIATION

Kabeljou (kob), snoek or angelfish may be used instead of hake.

HINT

To skin tomatoes, pour boiling water over and set aside for a while. The skins will peel off easily.

'Aunt' Baby's tomato-fish dish

Fish bobotie

6–8 SERVINGS

In the old days, people cooked this bobotie in a greased saucepan on top of the stove, says Auntie Martha Solomon, but now it's baked in the oven.

4–6 maasbankers (horse mackerel) or any white fish such as hake, skinned
1 onion
1 clove garlic
2 sprigs fresh parsley, chopped
1 chilli
1 carrot, peeled
2 potatoes, peeled
1 egg
1 t (5 ml) grated nutmeg
1 t (5 ml) turmeric
2 t (10 ml) curry powder
1 t (5 ml) salt
3 T (45 ml) vinegar or lemon juice

Preheat the oven to 180 °C.

Mince the fish, onion, garlic, parsley, chilli, carrot and potatoes in a mincer or food processor. Add the remaining ingredients and mix well. Spoon into a large, greased ovenproof dish and level the top. Bake for 35–40 minutes, until golden brown and cooked. Serve with white rice and pampoenmoes (breaded pumpkin) (see page 112).

INA'S HINT: Beat 2 eggs into 1 c (250 ml) buttermilk and season with salt, lemon pepper or black pepper. Pour over the bobotie before baking.

Fishcakes

4–5 SERVINGS

The West Coast is the home of the fishcake, and every cook believes hers is the best. The following recipe comes from Helen Arendse.

250 g hake fillets
250 g haddock fillets
3 slices day-old bread
1 small onion, grated
3 T (45 ml) chopped fresh parsley
1 t (5 ml) freshly ground black pepper
1 egg, lightly beaten
2 t (10 ml) grated nutmeg (or less, if preferred)
1 t (5 ml) oil
1 t (5 ml) vinegar
1 t (5 ml) salt
oil for pan-frying

Poach the hake and haddock fillets in a little water for about 10 minutes. Drain well and flake. Soak the bread in water or milk for 5 minutes, then squeeze out the excess liquid. Mix the flaked fish and bread with the rest of the ingredients and shape into cakes. Pan-fry in oil until golden brown. Serve with white rice and braised tomatoes and onions.

HINT

For a crisp outer layer, dip the fishcakes in flour before frying.

Fish bobotie with a topping of eggs, buttermilk and seasoning

Barbel rissoles

6–8 SERVINGS

Barbel is not as popular as it once was. It's a very ugly and slimy fish, which is why it is no longer widely eaten. If it's cleaned correctly and thoroughly, however, it's just as tasty as any other fish, says Aunt Tottie Cloete.

4 barbel (or 1 kg hake, if preferred)
1 onion
salt and pepper to taste
1–2 eggs
cake flour
oil for pan-frying

Wash the slime off the barbel completely in hot water. Cut out the backbone and entrails. Skin and fillet the fish and wash it again. Mince finely or chop the flesh in a food processor. Grate the onion and add to the fish. Season with salt and pepper. Roll into balls, dip in beaten egg and then in flour. Heat the oil in a pan and fry the fish rissoles until golden brown. Serve with rice.

HINT

Be careful when cleaning the fish, as it can be painful if the bones stick into your hands. The heads can be used to make a delicious soup. Barbel is sometimes used to make a 'kortkerrie' (fish head curry) (see page 48).

Favourite fishcakes

12–18 SERVINGS

The cloves and nutmeg add a marvellous spiciness to Johanna Coetzee's fish cakes. Most West Coast people still have a mincer, which works by turning a handle, but a food processor can be used to chop the fish, and the vegetables may be grated instead of minced.

4 maasbankers or mackerel
2 tomatoes, skinned
2 onions, quartered
2 carrots, peeled
2 cloves garlic
6 slices day-old bread
2 t (10 ml) vinegar
½ t (2,5 ml) ground cloves
1 t (5 ml) grated nutmeg
salt and pepper to taste
2 T (30 ml) chopped fresh parsley
1 T (15 ml) chutney
2 eggs, beaten
cake flour
oil for pan-frying

Skin and bone the fish. Mince the fish alternately with the vegetables and 4 slices bread in a mincer (no. 8 plate). Lastly, mince the remaining bread. Add the vinegar, seasonings, parsley and chutney to the fish mixture and mix well. Add the eggs and mix well. Shape into fishcakes, roll in flour and fry in hot oil until golden brown. Serve with white rice and vegetables, or fresh bread and jam.

VARIATION

Canned pilchards or any other canned fish, except sardines packed in oil, may be used instead of fresh fish.

HINT

If the fish are larger than average, remember to increase the quantities of the other ingredients.

Favourite fish cakes

Lientjie Vraagom's fishcakes

10–12 FISH CAKES

Fishcakes taste even better if prepared the day before, because they've stood overnight and all the flavours have developed.

1 kg whole hake
5 medium potatoes, peeled
4 slices fresh bread or 1½ c (375 ml) fresh white breadcrumbs
2 onions, grated
2 eggs, beaten
2 t (10 ml) lemon juice
1 t (5 ml) salt
½ t (2,5 ml) cayenne pepper
oil for pan-frying

Boil the fish in enough water to cover it, for 10–12 minutes, until just cooked. Drain and cool. Remove the skin and bones and flake the fish with two forks. Boil the potatoes until tender, then drain and mash. Add the mashed potatoes, bread or breadcrumbs, grated onions, eggs, lemon juice and seasonings to the fish. Mix well and shape into cakes. Fry in moderately hot oil until golden brown. Serve with white rice and vegetables.

HINTS

For a starter, make smaller fish cakes.

The fish cakes may be rolled in a little flour and refrigerated for 30 minutes to firm up before frying.

Maasbanker fishcakes

6–8 SERVINGS

The recipe for these tasty maasbanker (horse mackerel) fishcakes comes from Lenie Talmakkies.

4 maasbankers or mackerel
2 onions, coarsely chopped
2 tomatoes, skinned and quartered
2 carrots, peeled and thickly sliced
2 cloves garlic, crushed
6 slices bread or 2 c (500 ml) fresh breadcrumbs
2 t (10 ml) vinegar
½ t (2,5 ml) ground cloves
2 t (10 ml) salt
1 t (5 ml) pepper
1 T (15 ml) chutney
2 T (30 ml) chopped fresh parsley
2 eggs, beaten
cake flour
oil for pan-frying

Skin and bone the uncooked fish. Finely mince the fish, vegetables and slices of bread alternately in a mincer, ending with a slice of bread. If chopping the fish in a food processor, use breadcrumbs. Add the vinegar, seasonings, chutney and parsley to the fish mixture and mix well. Add the eggs. Shape into cakes and roll in flour. Fry in hot oil until golden brown. Serve with mashed potatoes with tomato and onion smoor.

VARIATION

This recipe may also be used to make ordinary rissoles – use 550 g lean beef mince instead of fish.

The off season is often a time of unemployment for fishermen.

When the catch was good and money was therefore more plentiful, meat was on the menu. 'Bredies' (stews) were always popular, as were 'oumens onder die kombers' (stuffed cabbage leaves), 'veldkoolbredie' (wild asparagus stew), 'kerrie-afval' (curried tripe) and liver in sour sauce.

MEAT
FOR THE POT ...

Oumens onder die kombers

4–5 SERVINGS

The recipe for stuffed cabbage leaves and its variations are found in virtually every food culture. The nutmeg adds a distinctly spicy flavour to this West Coast 'frikkadel' (rissole) favourite.

1 large cabbage, separated into leaves and the stalk discarded
2 T (30 ml) oil
1 onion, finely chopped
450 g beef mince
1 egg
1 t (5 ml) salt
½ t (2,5 ml) freshly ground peppercorns
2 cloves garlic, crushed
2 slices day-old bread, soaked in water
½ t (2,5 ml) grated nutmeg

ONION LAYER
3 T (45 ml) oil
2 onions, chopped
salt, sugar and pepper to taste

Preheat the oven to 180 °C. Pour boiling water over the cabbage leaves and set aside.

Heat the oil in a frying pan, add the onion and fry until browned. Mix the mince, egg, salt, pepper, garlic and fried onion together in a mixing bowl. Squeeze the water out of the bread and add the bread to the meat mixture. Mix to a loose texture. Drain the cabbage leaves and set aside. Shape the mince mixture into frikkadels and wrap each one neatly in a cabbage leaf.

For the onion layer, heat the oil, add the onions and fry until golden brown. Season to taste. Place the fried onion in an ovenproof glass dish and place the cabbage frikkadels on top. Cover and bake for 40–45 minutes. Remove from the oven and sprinkle nutmeg over. Serve hot. Delicious with beetroot salad.

VARIATION

SWEET-AND-SOUR CURRIED FRIKKADELS
1 T (15 ml) curry powder
1 T (15 ml) turmeric
2 t (10 ml) vinegar
1 t (5 ml) sugar
1 c (250 ml) water
salt to taste

Preheat the oven to 180 °C. Make the frikkadels as described above, but without the cabbage leaves. Cook all the ingredients for the curry sauce together for 15 minutes. Place the frikkadels on the fried onion layer in an ovenproof glass dish and cover with curry sauce. Bake for 40–45 minutes.

HINT

Both stuffed cabbage leaves and sweet-and-sour curried frikkadels may be served with yellow rice or mashed potatoes and green peas.

INA'S HINT: There are no shortcuts for cooking the onions – those for the frikkadel mixture and the onion layer must be cooked until well browned.

Time spent with family is precious to fishermen who are away from home for long periods.

Mince vetkoekies

4 SERVINGS

Pauline Moses says cooked chicken or fish may be used instead of the mince in this recipe. 'Vetkoekies' (scone or bread dough deep-fried in hot oil) are a great favourite among the fishermen when they are at sea.

1 c (250 ml) cake flour
1 t (5 ml) baking powder
a pinch of salt
½ t (2,5 ml) pepper
1 large egg, beaten
½ c (125 ml) milk
1 c (250 ml) cooked beef mince
½ c (125 ml) oil

Sift the flour, baking powder and salt together and add the pepper. Beat the egg and milk together and add to the mince. Mix the flour mixture gradually into the mince mixture and stir until the batter is thick and smooth. It must have a dropping consistency and not be too thick. Heat the oil in a pan over moderate heat. Drop spoonfuls of batter into the hot oil and deep fry until golden brown.

Meatloaf with a potato topping

10–12 SERVINGS

This is an economical dish that tastes even better the following day.

MEATLOAF
1 kg beef mince
1 c (250 ml) soft, fresh white breadcrumbs
4 T (60 ml) chopped fresh parsley
1 onion, finely grated
1 clove garlic, crushed
2 eggs, beaten
2 T (30 ml) tomato sauce
1 t (5 ml) salt
2 t (10 ml) pepper
a pinch of ground cloves

POTATO TOPPING
3 c (750 ml) water
1 t (5 ml) salt
8–10 potatoes, peeled and cubed
1 t (5 ml) pepper
2 egg yolks or 2 T (30 ml) butter
½ c (125 ml) grated cheese
½ t (2,5 ml) paprika

Preheat the oven to 180 °C.

Place all the ingredients for the meatloaf in a mixing bowl and mix lightly with a fork. Turn the mixture out into a greased loaf pan and level the surface. Bake for 45 minutes.

For the topping, bring the water and salt to the boil, add the potatoes and cook until soft. Drain. Mash the potatoes, season with pepper and add the egg yolks or butter.

Increase the oven temperature to 200 °C.

Turn the meatloaf out onto an ovenproof serving platter. Cover the entire loaf, right round and on top, with the potato mixture and sprinkle cheese and paprika over. Return to the oven and bake for 20–25 minutes, until golden brown. Serve hot with cooked vegetables.

Vetkoekies prepared with seasoned, leftover mince

Samp and beans with beef

8 SERVINGS

This deliciously savoury recipe from Joan Esau of Goedverwacht is perfect for stilling hunger pangs.

1 packet (500 g) samp
1 packet (500 g) dried beans
8 c (2 litres) cold water
1 onion, chopped
1 kg beef, cubed
2 T (30 ml) oil
6 whole cloves
salt and pepper to taste

Soak the samp and beans overnight, in 1 litre water each, in separate containers.

Cook the samp and beans separately in fresh water, as they take the same length of time to cook. Drain.

Braise the onion and meat in oil until browned and add the whole cloves. Add the drained samp and beans. Add as much water as is needed, depending on whether you want a thin or a thick gravy. Add salt and pepper and simmer until done.

Kerrie-afval with samp

6 SERVINGS

If you are fond of tripe, 'kerrie-afval' (curried tripe) with samp is a feast. Invite a few tripe lovers over to enjoy the meal with you.

1 packet (500 g) samp
8 c (2 litres) cold water
⅖ c (100 ml) sugar
5 T (75 ml) butter or margarine
1 t (5 ml) salt
2 cow's feet or 4–6 sheep's trotters
1 sheep's tripe
3 onions, sliced
2 large potatoes
1 T (15 ml) curry powder
1 t (5 ml) turmeric
2 t (10 ml) vinegar
2 t (10 ml) sugar
salt and pepper to taste

Soak the samp overnight in cold water. The next day, cook the samp slowly in fresh water until tender. Add the sugar, butter or margarine, and salt and mash lightly with a large fork.

Prepare the offal by cutting out the glands between the 'toes' and then shaving or burning off the hairs of the feet or trotters. Clean the tripe thoroughly and cut it in pieces. Cover the offal with water.

Add the onions to the offal and cook slowly for 3–4 hours. Peel and cut each potato into 4–6 pieces and add to the offal. Add the remaining ingredients and cook until the potatoes are tender. Serve with the samp.

HINT

Caroline Talmakkies suggests that 8 apricot halves be cooked with the tripe and, if apricots are not available, that chutney or apricot jam to taste be added just before serving.

INA'S HINT: After cutting the tripe, soak it for 20 minutes in water to which 2 t (10 ml) bicarbonate of soda has been added. This will neutralise the acidic digestive juices.

Pan-fried liver in sour sauce

5–6 SERVINGS

LIVER
1 kg sheep or ox liver
4 T (60 ml) vinegar
½ c (125 ml) cold water
salt and pepper to taste
cake flour
oil for pan-frying

SOUR SAUCE
½ c (125 ml) water
4 T (60 ml) vinegar
1 t (5 ml) sugar
salt and pepper to taste

Clean the liver, remove and discard the membrane and cut the liver into slices. Marinate for 1 hour in a mixture of vinegar and water. Drain and season with salt and pepper. Roll the liver in flour and pan-fry in shallow, medium-hot oil. Remove from the pan, place in an ovenproof dish and keep warm.

Now make the sauce in the pan in which the liver was fried. First pour off all the oil. Loosen the pan scrapings by cooking the water and vinegar in the pan until the mixture thickens. Add sugar to taste to remove most of the sourness. Season with salt and pepper. When the sauce is nice and thick, pour it over the liver and serve immediately with mashed potatoes and fresh tomatoes.

Zelda Williams' mother always serves this dish on a Saturday as a light meal before the more festive Sunday fare.

Sheep's ribs with porridge and potatoes

6 SERVINGS

750 g sheep's ribs
4 c (1 litre) water
2 t (10 ml) salt
1 T (15 ml) black pepper
3 T (45 ml) butter or margarine
4 c (1 litre) skimmed milk
½ c (125 ml) cake flour
6 potatoes, peeled and cubed
salt and pepper to taste

Boil the ribs, water and salt in a heavy-based saucepan until tender; this will take approximately 90 minutes. Remove the ribs, reserve the salted water, season with black pepper and bake for 30 minutes, uncovered, in the oven at 180 °C.

Place the butter or margarine and 3 c (750 ml) of milk in a saucepan and heat to just below boiling point. Make a paste of cake flour and remaining milk and stir it into the hot milk in the saucepan, until the porridge thickens. Season. Boil the potatoes in the water in which the ribs were cooked, until just tender. Serve the rib with the cooked potatoes and porridge.

HINTS

Replace the flour with 400 ml polenta to make the porridge.
Sheep's ribs are delicious with a tomato and onion salad.

Quiet times are used for activities such as net repairs.

This dish will revitalize a fisherman who's exhausted from a hard day's work. Because fishermen have such a hard physical life, it's every mother's dream that her children will receive an education so that they will not be at the mercy of the capricious sea.

Sheep's ribs served with polenta and a tomato and onion salad

Veldkoolbredie

6–8 SERVINGS

'Veldkool', or wild asparagus (*Tracheandra* sp.), grows in the veld on the West Coast. There are two kinds: the broad leafed and narrow leafed ('slangkoppie'). These plants grow sparsely, and it's difficult to gather enough for a meal, so the broad leaf is preferred. 'Veldkool', also known locally as 'hotnotskool', first appears after the June rains. The light-green stalks must be picked before September. Once the delicate white flowers appear on the stalk, it becomes inedible. Aunt Tottie Cloete's mother taught her to add chopped 'surings' (a local veld species of sorrel, with a yellow flower) to the 'veldkoolbredie' (wild asparagus stew). Wild garlic, which removes the wild taste from 'veldkool', grows in the hills all along the West Coast and is particularly plentiful in winter.

1 kg veldkool (wild asparagus) or asparagus
2 large onions, sliced
oil for pan-frying
1 kg mutton or lamb shin or neck
4 medium potatoes, peeled and quartered
1 bunch surings
½ c (125 ml) chicken stock
salt and pepper to taste

If using veldkool, remove the stalks – the edible part that looks like asparagus – and steep them in a strong salt and water solution for 10 minutes to remove any insects. Rinse well.

Boil the veldkool or asparagus in water for 5 minutes. Drain it in a colander, placing a heavy object, such as a saucer, on top to squeeze out all the water.

Meanwhile, fry the onions in oil until browned, then add the meat and braise until golden brown and parcooked. Add the potatoes and cook for 10 minutes. Add the veldkool or asparagus, surings, stock and seasonings, and stew until the potatoes are done. Serve with rice.

VARIATION

Use broccoli or *waterblommetjies* ('little water flowers' – a species of *Aponogeton distachyos*) instead of veldkool.

HINTS

Use 1 T (15 ml) vinegar, sorrel (a herb), or freshly squeezed lemon juice instead of the surings. If necessary, add a little more stock to moisten the bredie (stew).

Aunt Tottie on her wedding day. She notes that it's quite a sight to see people gathering 'hotnotskool' from July to September, and says humorously: 'Kyk hoe wei hulle al weer in die veld' (Look at them 'grazing' again in the veld).

Veldkoolbredie prepared with asparagus

It can become really hot on the West Coast, even though the adjoining sea is cold and on those stiflingly hot days a cool salad with a meal is always welcome. But that doesn't mean that salads may only be served in summer – sometimes a spicy salad is the perfect choice to accompany a warm winter dish.

SALADS FOR SUMMER

Curried noodle salad

8 SERVINGS

6 c (1,5 litres) water
1 packet (500 g) noodles
2 t (10 ml) salt
1 t (5 ml) turmeric
1 large sweet pepper, chopped
1 large tomato, chopped
1 large onion, chopped

SALAD DRESSING

1 c (250 ml) oil
1 c (250 ml) sugar
1 c (250 ml) tomato sauce
1 c (250 ml) vinegar
6 T (90 ml) curry powder

Bring the water to boiling point and add the noodles, salt and turmeric. Boil according to packet instructions until just tender. Drain and pour cold water over to stop the cooking process and separate the noodles. Add the sweet pepper, tomato and onion to the cooled noodles and mix. For the dressing, mix the oil, sugar, tomato sauce and vinegar together well and pour the dressing over the noodles. Add the curry powder and mix well. Leave to stand for a few hours before serving.

INA'S HINT: Fry the curry powder in 4 T (60 ml) of the oil until cooked and full of flavour before adding it to the other ingredients.

Mercia Hans (nee Julius), Dorothea Rosant (nee Jantjies) and a friend from Goedverwacht enjoying New Year's Day on the beach. Spending this day on the beach was a tradition and families went well prepared for the picnic meal, which included salads.

This economical salad may be prepared well ahead of time and is a perfect accompaniment to braaied (barbecued) meat.

Curried noodle salad

Beetroot salad

6 SERVINGS

This homemade beetroot salad is delicious served with 'oumens onder die kombers' (stuffed cabbage leaves) (see page 68) or cabbage bredie (cabbage stew).

3 c (750 ml) water
½ t (2,5 ml) salt
1 bunch beetroot – leave 5 cm of the stalk attached to the root
1 onion, grated
sugar to taste
½ c (125 ml) brown vinegar

Boil the water and salt together. Wash the beetroot thoroughly and place in the boiling salted water. Boil until the skin is soft and can be pulled off easily. Slice or grate the beetroot and place in a salad bowl. Add the onion, sugar and vinegar. Chill.

INA'S HINT: Beetroot leaves are delicious cooked with spinach.

Pineapple salad

5 SERVINGS

This unusual combination of ingredients makes for a very tasty salad.

1 t (5 ml) sugar
½ t (2,5 ml) salt
1 T (15 ml) oil
2 T (30 ml) lemon juice
1 pineapple, peeled and grated
1 onion, soaked in boiling water and finely chopped
1 clove garlic, crushed

Mix the sugar, salt, oil and lemon juice together. Mix the pineapple, onion and garlic, then pour the lemon mixture over the pineapple mixture. Serve this salad at any fish or meat braai.

Ouma Anna Mitchell from Laaiplek worked in a fish factory for many years. She openly shared her experience of women's hardship in this environment.

Sousboontjies

6–8 SERVINGS

1 packet (500 g) sugar beans
6 c (1,5 litres) boiling water
½ c (125 ml) sugar
1 t (5 ml) salt
½ c (125 ml) vinegar
1 T (15 ml) butter or margarine
2 t (10 ml) cake flour
2 t (10 ml) cornflour
2 t (10 ml) custard powder

Cover the beans with boiling water and leave to soak overnight. Pour off the water and cook the beans in 4 c (1 litre) fresh water until just tender. Drain, cover with 1½ c (375 ml) cold water and set aside for 30 minutes. Add the sugar, salt, vinegar and butter or margarine. Stir well and bring to boiling point over low heat. Boil the beans until completely soft and remove from the heat. Mix the flour, cornflour and custard powder with ½ c (125 ml) water and stir into the beans. Cook until thickened. Serve cold, with braaied (barbecued) meat or fried fish.

INA'S HINT: Bottled 'sousboontjies' keep very well in the refrigerator. They also freeze successfully.

In an old Afrikaans song, Al Debbo sings: 'Sousboontjies is so reg na my smaak ...' (bean salad is precisely what I like). What more can you say?

Tomato sambal

6 SERVINGS

1 large onion, finely chopped
1 sweet pepper, finely chopped
2 large ripe tomatoes, chopped
1 chilli, finely chopped
4 T (60 ml) white vinegar
½ t (2,5 ml) salt
1 t (5 ml) sugar

Mix all the ingredients together. Chill for 1 hour. Serve with breyani, curry or pan-fried fish.

Snoek and chips salad

6 SERVINGS

1 lettuce
200 g freshly made potato chips
1 onion, sliced into rings
2 tomatoes, chopped
2–4 hard-boiled eggs, sliced
500 g cooked snoek, flaked
5 T (75 ml) lemon juice
1 t (5 ml) mustard powder
1 c (250 ml) fresh cream
6 whole radishes

Line a salad bowl or platter with lettuce leaves. Layer chips, onion rings, tomatoes, egg and snoek on top of the lettuce leaves. Sprinkle lemon juice over. Mix the mustard and cream and pour it over the salad. Garnish with radishes.

Fish and chips West Coast style.

TOP: *A typical West Coast fisherman's cottage.*
BOTTOM: *The Paternoster Hotel – a popular West Coast landmark.*

It is said that kneading dough calms the spirit ... Besides, nothing can beat the aroma of bread while it is baking, and few things are quite as delicious as warm, freshly baked bread with butter and jam. Comfort food? This is the real thing!

OUR DAILY BREAD ...

Buttermilk bread

MAKES 1 LOAF

3½ c (875 ml) self-raising flour, sifted
1 t (5 ml) salt
2 c (500 ml) buttermilk
4 T (60 ml) water

Preheat the oven to 180 °C. Place all the ingredients except the water in a bowl and mix them to a slack dough, using a wooden spoon. Rinse out the buttermilk container with the water and add it to the dough. Turn out into a greased loaf pan; the pan must be three-quarters full. Bake for 40–45 minutes. Leave to cool in the pan for 10 minutes, then turn the loaf out onto a wire rack to cool completely.

VARIATION

To make a beer bread, replace the buttermilk with 1 can or bottle (340 ml) beer.

This quick-mix loaf, eaten warm from the oven with butter and apricot jam, is delectable with fried snoek or galjoen.

Yellow pumpkin bread

MAKES 1 LOAF

2 c (500 ml) cake flour
2 t (10 ml) baking powder
½ t (2,5 ml) salt
a pinch of bicarbonate of soda
½ c (125 ml) sugar
1 c (250 ml) cooked pumpkin, mashed
2 eggs, beaten
4 T (60 ml) oil

Preheat the oven to 180 °C.

Sift the flour, baking powder, salt and bicarbonate of soda together. Stir in the sugar. Mix the mashed pumpkin with the eggs and oil, then add to the flour mixture and mix to form a moist dough. Turn out into a greased loaf pan and bake for 50 minutes. Leave to stand for 10 minutes to cool down, then turn out onto a wire rack.

This loaf is often served on Sundays, with the midday meal. It is delicious with fish.

Quick raisin bread

MAKES 1 LOAF

2 c (500 ml) self-raising flour, sifted
1 c (250 ml) raisins
1 c (250 ml) sugar
2 t (10 ml) aniseed
2 eggs
1–1½ c (250–375 ml) milk

Preheat the oven to 180 °C. Mix the flour, raisins, sugar and aniseed together. Add the eggs, one at a time, and mix well with a wooden spoon. Stir in enough milk to make a slack dough. Turn out into a greased medium-sized loaf pan and bake for 30–40 minutes. Serve with butter and jam or grated cheese.

This quick loaf combines the traditional flavours of aniseed and raisins. Delicious with a cup of coffee or any typically West Coast meal.

Soetsuurdeegbrood

MAKES 4 LOAVES

YEAST MIXTURE
8 c (2 litres) water
1 t (5 ml) salt
1 t (5 ml) sugar
2 potatoes, unpeeled
3 c (750 ml) bread flour
1 c (250 ml) boiling water

BREAD
2,5 kg bread flour
1 T (15 ml) salt

To make the yeast, heat the water for the yeast in a saucepan until lukewarm. Remove the saucepan from the stove, add the salt and sugar and stir until dissolved. Cut the potatoes, peel and all, into thick slices and add to the lukewarm water. Stir 2 c (500 ml) flour into the potato and water mixture. Cover with a plastic bag. Wrap tightly in newspaper and leave in a warm place overnight.

The next morning, add the boiling water and remaining flour to the yeast mixture and beat well. Cover again with a plastic bag and newspaper and leave in a warm place until the afternoon. The yeast mixture will have risen, and will be ready for kneading. Remove the potato slices from the yeast.

For the bread, place the bread flour and salt in an enamel basin. Make a hollow in the centre and add the yeast mixture. Knead until the dough is soft and elastic and no longer sticks to your hands. Fill greased loaf pans to three-quarters full with dough. Cover and leave to rise until the loaf pans are full.

Bake for 50 minutes in an oven preheated to 200 °C, until golden brown. Allow to cool slightly before turning out onto a wire rack to cool completely.

HINT
For a soft crust, spread butter or margarine on top of the loaves while they are still warm.

INA'S HINTS: To dry out the base, remove the loaves from the pans 10 minutes before the end of the baking time, and continue baking. If you want to reserve a 'yeast starter' for future baking, refrigerate 2 c (500 ml) of the yeast mixture and replace with 2 c (500 ml) lukewarm water when kneading the bread.

'Soetsuurdeegbrood' (salt-rising yeast bread) is very popular, and is usually snapped up first at bazaars. This recipe from Sanna van Wyk goes well with soup, or simply on its own, with jam or cheese.

Soetsuurdeegbrood

In years gone by, eating out of doors was not common along the West Coast. It was only in the mid-1980s that Sea Harvest began to package and sell 'braaisnoek' (snoek for barbecuing), but since then 'braaiing' (barbecuing) snoek has become increasingly popular. Other kinds of fish are now also 'braaied' out of doors.

IN THE OPEN AIR

Snoek over the coals

8–10 SERVINGS

This recipe, from Cecil Stoffberg, has for many years provided a popular, inexpensive, yet delicious meal. The apricot sauce is marvellous and very typical of the West Coast.

1 snoek, salted beforehand
pepper to taste

APRICOT BASTING SAUCE
4 T (60 ml) mayonnaise
4 T (60 ml) garlic butter
4 T (60 ml) smooth apricot jam

MAYO BASTING SAUCE
1 c (250 ml) mayonnaise
6 T (90 ml) butter or margarine

Cut the ready-salted snoek into portions and sprinkle with pepper. Heat the ingredients for the basting sauce of your choice over low heat and mix well. Using a small brush, brush the fish with the sauce. Braai the fish over glowing coals – the coals must not be too hot – until the fish comes easily off the bone. Serve with fresh bread and a salad, or a toasted tomato and onion sandwich.

VARIATION

The snoek may also be baked in the oven, with either of the basting sauces.

HINT

Inexperienced braaiers will find the mayo basting sauce easier and they can be sure that the cooked fish will be tender and juicy without the danger that it will burn. The flavour of the apricot basting sauce is delicious, but one has to take care that it doesn't burn. Make sure the heat from the coals is moderate.

The Sea Dove *fishing off the Saldanha Bay harbour, Hoedjiesbaai.*

Before echo-sounding equipment was used to track down fish, fishermen did not put out to sea at night for the period when the moon was full (about a week). At full moon, the fish see better, which makes catching them more difficult. The period of the full moon was 'pay' time, and fishermen were paid at the start of the period. With the arrival of echo-sounding and radar equipment, 'pay' time moved to the end of the month.

Snoek over the coals

Galjoen over the coals

6 SERVINGS

This is Eric Wilsnach's favourite fish recipe. Many West Coast people joined the South African war effort during the Second World War, and went to fight in North Africa and Italy. This typical West Coast dish is probably the one dish from home that they often missed most.

1–2 galjoen (depending on size)
coarse salt
pepper to taste
lemon pepper

First butterfly the galjoen, then sprinkle coarse salt over. After 15 minutes, rinse the salt off thoroughly. Leave the galjoen to drip until dry.

Sprinkle the pepper and lemon pepper over. Braai the fish slowly over the coals – the coals must not be too hot. Start on the flesh side, and end on the skin side. Turn once only and season lightly. Serve with fresh bread and apricot jam.

VARIATION
Galjoen can be brushed with a mixture of the following: the juice of 1 lemon, ½ c (125 ml) mayonnaise and 4 T (60 ml) melted garlic butter.

Galjoen bite when the sea has a slight swell – not too rough and not too still – and the tide must be rising. The water must also be 'troebel' (choppy).

Malmok braai

For those who do not know, a 'malmok' (mollymawk) is a kind of seabird, and is fried as you would chicken. When the fishermen out at sea did not catch any fish, they had to find something to eat and so they caught 'malmoks'. The bird is caught at sea, using a fishing line and a triangular piece of iron on which bait is placed. The 'malmok' picks up the bait and in this way is caught. 'Malmok' braai was a sought-after Sunday meal, especially in times when fish were scarce. Traditionally, the bird was left overnight in brine after plucking and cleaning. It was fried with potatoes and onions and then slowly simmered. Sweetened samp and raisins or sweetened barley were favourite accompaniments. But be warned: today the 'malmok' is a protected bird and may no longer be caught.

Toepens harders

6 SERVINGS

The scales of these 'toepens' harders (whole mullet) are not removed. To find out when the fish is ready, watch the eyes. While the fish is cooking, the eyes swell up; remove the fish from the grid just after the eyes have burst.

6 harders (mullet)
1 packet (250 g) coarse salt

Wash the harders and roll the wet fish in coarse salt. Set aside for 30 minutes.

Make the fire, using dry wood that will make good coals. When the coals are ready, shake the salt lightly from the harders and braai them over the coals until cooked. Serve with bread and korrelkonfyt (grape jam).

VARIATION

Prepare the harders as described in the recipe. Heat oil in a pan, shake the salt from the harders and fry them until done.

A horse-drawn cart beside the canteen in Langebaan, April 1916.

Christin and Leen's fish potjie

12 SERVINGS

The secret of this 'potjie' (three-legged, cast-iron pot recipe) is not to stir the contents after the fish and other seafood have been added.

3 T (45 ml) oil
3 onions, sliced into rings
1 sweet pepper, chopped
3 cloves garlic, cut into strips
5 medium potatoes, cubed
water
1 kg hake, cubed
1 kg mussels in the shell, rinsed well
1 kg calamari, cut into rings
1 kg crab sticks (optional)
2 t (10 ml) celery salt
2 t (10 ml) pepper

Heat the oil in a 'potjie' (three-legged, cast-iron pot), add the onion and fry until softened. Add the sweet pepper and garlic and stir-fry lightly. Add the potatoes, cover with a lid and braise slowly until just done. Add small quantities of water as needed. Add all the fish and seafood, cover with a lid and simmer for 5 minutes. Season with celery salt and pepper and simmer for a further 5 minutes. Serve on a bed of rice.

VARIATION

Frozen mixed seafood may be used instead of fresh.

Curried fish potjie

10–15 SERVINGS

Because cooking times of the fish and seafood vary, they should not be added to this fish 'potjie' at the same time. Hake and mussels will disintegrate if they are cooked too quickly, and calamari gets tough if overcooked. Do not stir the 'potjie' too often.

⅖ c (100 ml) oil
3 onions, chopped
3 cloves garlic, chopped
1 sweet pepper, peeled and chopped
1 kg potatoes, peeled and cubed
water
2 T (30 ml) curry powder
1 t (5 ml) vinegar
1 kg hake, cubed
1 kg mussels, in the shell, rinsed well
salt and pepper to taste
1 stalk celery, finely chopped,
or 2 T (30 ml) dried celery
1 kg calamari, cut into rings

Heat the oil in a 'potjie', add the onions and garlic and then the sweet pepper. Stir-fry for 5 minutes. Add the potatoes and cook until done, adding small quantities of water if necessary. Add the curry powder and vinegar. After 10 minutes, add the hake, then add the mussels. Season with salt and pepper, add the celery and calamari and simmer for about 5 minutes, until done. Serve with white rice.

VARIATION

Frozen seafood mix may be used instead of fresh.

Curried fish potjie

Crayfish potjie

6–8 SERVINGS

4 whole crayfish
3 large onions, chopped
6 T (90 ml) oil
1 large sweet pepper, chopped
2 large tomatoes, skinned and chopped
1 T (15 ml) crushed garlic
1 T (15 ml) finely grated fresh ginger
2 T (30 ml) '13-in-one' curry mix
1 kg potatoes, peeled and cubed
½ c (125 ml) water
1 t (5 ml) salt
500 g crab sticks or kingklip, cubed

Remove the crayfish meat from the shell and legs and cut into pieces. In a 'potjie', braise the onions in a little oil, then add the sweet pepper, tomatoes, garlic, ginger and curry mix and braise for 10 minutes. Add the potatoes to the curry mix. Add the water and salt and cook until the potatoes are just tender. Add the crayfish and simmer for 5 minutes. Add the crab sticks or fish and simmer for a further 5 minutes. Serve with white rice.

HINT

Parboil the crayfish for 2 minutes before shelling– the meat will come away easily from the shell and it will also retain its shape.

A view of boats fishing for crayfish off Lambert's Bay, with a suspended basket loaded with crayfish in the foreground c. 1925.

In the past, whenever crayfish was scarce, people used only the 'bakke' (the body, head and legs) and sold the tails. Nowadays, the crayfish are too small and there isn't enough meat in the legs to make it worth the effort to remove it.

Crayfish potjie

William Joshua's fish potjie

8–10 SERVINGS

1 octopus
2 whole crayfish
⅖ c (100 ml) oil
4–5 large onions, chopped
2 large sweet peppers, chopped
4 t (20 ml) crushed garlic
4 t (20 ml) grated fresh ginger
1 kg potatoes
2 c (500 ml) water
2 t (10 ml) flavour enhancer (Aromat®)
2 t (10 ml) black pepper
1 chilli, thinly sliced
1 kg kingklip or hake, cleaned and cut into portions
3 large tomatoes, grated
500 g calamari rings
500 g mussel meat
500 g small prawns

Turn the octopus head inside out and remove the ink and entrails. Dry it on the rocks or hang it on the wash line for about 2 hours to ensure it dries thoroughly. Then remove the skin with shears, rinse the octopus and cut the tentacles and head into 5 cm-long portions.

To clean the crayfish, break the tail from the body with a turn-and-pull motion. Halve the tail lengthways and remove the alimentary canal. Break open the body and remove the poison bag near the feelers. Cut the meat into portions and remove the meat from the legs.

Heat the oil in a 'potjie', sauté the onions, add the sweet peppers and braise until tender. Add the crushed garlic and ginger and stir well. Peel and cube the potatoes (not too small) and add them to the 'potjie' with 1 c (250 ml) water and the seasoning and chilli. Cook for 15 minutes.

Add the crayfish and fish, but do not stir. Cook for 5 minutes. Add the octopus and grated tomatoes and cook for a further 10 minutes. Add the calamari, mussels and prawns. Add the remaining water, if necessary, and cook for a further 5 minutes. Serve with white rice.

HINT

Chillies are less fiery if the seeds and membranes are removed.

Snoek being cleaned during the snoek season, St Helena Bay.

A delicious 'potjie' for those who want to spend the day on the beach.

Two men salting snoek at a table during the snoek season, St Helena Bay.

Potbrood

MAKES 1 BREAD

It's not every day that you get a recipe that says: 'Make a hole in the ground and line it with coals.' This recipe is the real thing! A flat-based, cast-iron pot is perfect for baking 'potbrood' (pot bread).

2 t (10 ml) sugar
1 packet (10 g) instant yeast
1 c (250 ml) lukewarm milk
2 T (30 ml) butter or margarine, melted
1 T (15 ml) cake flour
2 eggs, beaten
3½ c (875 ml) bread flour
2 t (10 ml) salt

Mix the sugar and yeast together. Add the milk, melted butter or margarine and cake flour and set aside for 10 minutes.

Add the eggs to the yeast mixture and mix well. Sift the bread flour and salt together. Add the yeast mixture to the flour and knead until the dough no longer sticks to your hands. Cover the dough with plastic and a thick layer of newspaper and leave to rise in a warm place for 25 minutes.

Knock the dough back and place in a greased cast-iron pot. Grease the inside of the lid, place the lid on the pot and leave to rise for a further 20 minutes.

Make a hole in the ground, line it with hot coals and place the pot in the hole. Place a few coals on the lid as well. Bake for 40–45 minutes. Place more coals on top if the coals get too cold. Delicious with butter or margarine and fig jam.

Roosterkoek

4 SERVINGS

What could be better than 'roosterkoek' (braai bread) cooked over glowing coals with fish fresh from the sea? When one sits around the fire, chatting, it's time to tell stories about the people of old, of storms at sea and the dramas and hardships that form part of a fisherman's life.

2 c (500 ml) cake or bread flour
½ t (2,5 ml) cream of tartar plus 1 t (5 ml) bicarbonate of soda, or 2½ t (12,5 ml) baking powder
1 t (5 ml) salt
4 T (60 ml) butter or margarine
½ c (125 ml) water
chopped fresh herbs (optional)

Sift the dry ingredients together. Rub the butter or margarine into the flour until the mixture looks like breadcrumbs. Add the water to the flour and mix to a soft dough. Roll the dough out on a floured surface to about 2 cm thick and cut into triangles. Sprinkle with chopped herbs if desired, then bake in an oven preheated to 180 °C or over moderately hot coals. Delicious with butter or margarine and jam.

INA'S HINT: The dough used to make 'soetsuurdeegbrood' (salt-rising yeast bread) on page 90 is ideal for roosterkoek, if you have the time.

Roosterkoek, sprinkled with chopped, fresh herbs

West Coast people are fond of sweet side dishes served with their meals. Bread and jam with fried fish is typically West Coast, and so are sweet potatoes – sweetened or baked in their skins. And where else in the world would you find sweetened barley and sweetened samp?

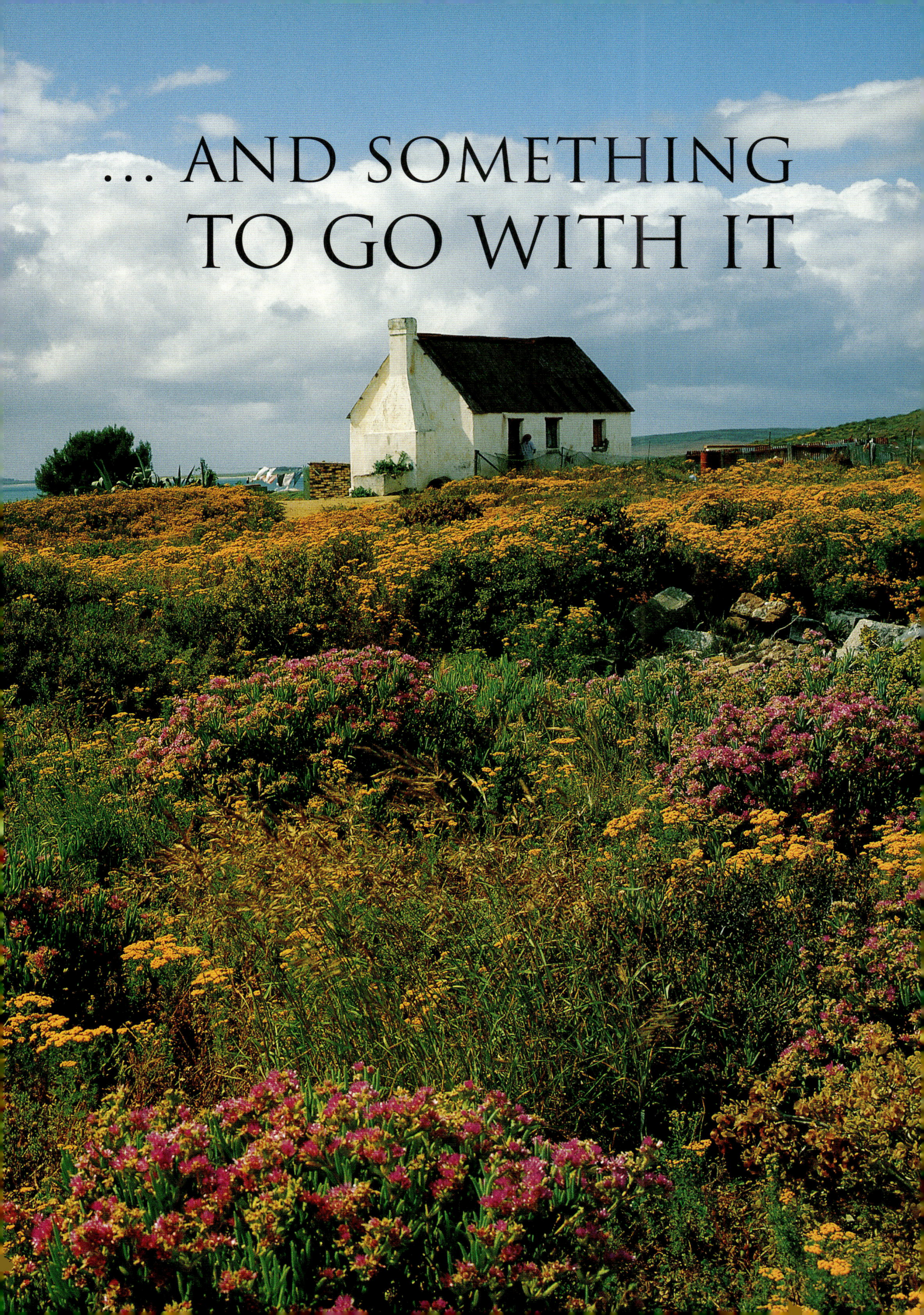

… AND SOMETHING TO GO WITH IT

Braised tomatoes and onions

4 SERVINGS

West Coast people enjoy this favourite sauce with pan-fried liver or fish.

3–4 large onions, chopped
2 T (30 ml) oil
1 T (15 ml) crushed garlic
3–4 large, ripe tomatoes, skinned and chopped
sugar to taste
1 t (5 ml) salt
1 t (5 ml) pepper

Sauté the onions in oil and add the garlic. Add the tomatoes, sugar, salt and pepper. Simmer slowly for about 20–30 minutes; stir from time to time until the sauce is cooked.

Dry spaghetti

6 SERVINGS

PASTA
4 c (1 litre) water
1 t (5 ml) salt
1 packet (500 g) spaghetti
1 T (15 ml) cooking or olive oil

SAUCE
3 T (45 ml) oil
1 large onion, chopped
3 cloves garlic, crushed
sugar to taste
½ t (2,5 ml) grated nutmeg
1 can (115 g) tomato paste

Bring the water and salt to the boil. Add the spaghetti and cook until tender. Drain, add oil and set aside.

To make the sauce, heat the oil, add the onion and sauté until transparent. Add the remaining ingredients and simmer until thoroughly mixed. Add the cooked spaghetti to the tomato sauce and stir with a wide-tined fork over low heat until all the spaghetti has been coated with tomato sauce. Serve with fried fish, mince rissoles or fried meat.

Every fishing community feels the influence of 'incomers'; people who come in from outside. Sometimes these 'incomers' come from as far away as overseas. Italian sailors, who had been shipwrecked off the West Coast, and stayed, left not only their DNA as an inheritance to the West Coast, but also this pasta dish. A typical Italian-style spaghetti, it has less sauce than a traditional Neapolitan, and is therefore referred to as 'dry'.

Dry spaghetti served with fresh herbs as a garnish

Yellow rice with raisins

4 SERVINGS

This is old-fashioned yellow rice at its best; a festive dish that is often eaten on Sundays.

1 c (250 ml) uncooked long-grain rice
2 c (500 ml) water
2 T (30 ml) butter or margarine
2 pieces stick cinnamon, broken into pieces
1 t (5 ml) turmeric
½ c (125 ml) sugar
½ c (125 ml) raisins

Place all the ingredients into a saucepan, bring to the boil and cook until the rice is tender. Drain in a colander, place over a saucepan of boiling water and steam for 15 minutes. Serve with fried meat or fish bobotie.

Savoury rice

6 SERVINGS

2 c (500 ml) uncooked rice
4 t (20 ml) chicken stock powder or garlic and herb seasoning
4 c (1 litre) cold water
1 T (15 ml) oil
1 onion, finely chopped
1 tomato, skinned and finely chopped
1 sweet pepper, finely chopped
salt and pepper to taste

Add the rice and stock powder or seasoning to the cold water, bring to the boil and cook until tender. Heat the oil, add the onion and sauté. Mix the tomato and sweet pepper with the braised onion, add to the cooked rice and season to taste. Serve with braaied meat or fried fish.

Cheryl Botha, now a grandmother, with her handsome partner, off to a wedding.

Sweet rice fritters

12 SERVINGS

This is the ideal way to use up leftover rice. In winter, it is popular as an accompaniment to fried food.

4 c (1 litre) cooked rice
1 c (250 ml) sugar
1 c (250 ml) milk
2 eggs, beaten
1 t (5 ml) vanilla essence
1 c (250 ml) self-raising flour, sifted
1 t (5 ml) grated nutmeg
oil for pan-frying

Mix the cooked rice and sugar in a mixing bowl. Mix the milk, eggs and vanilla and add to the rice. Mix well. Add the flour and nutmeg and mix. Heat the oil and drop spoonfuls of rice mixture in the hot oil. Fry until golden brown. Serve hot or cold.

Constance Maschilla (nee Julius) from Goedverwacht in 1965, well known for her sense of style, in typical Sunday dress.

Pampoenmoes

6–8 SERVINGS

½ large or 1 small pumpkin, peeled and thinly sliced
salt to taste
6–10 slices white bread (depending on the size of the pumpkin)
½ c (125 ml) butter or margarine
1 c (250 ml) sugar
6 pieces stick cinnamon, broken into small pieces
dried orange rind or the grated rind of 1 fresh orange
½ c (125 ml) water (depending on how dry the pumpkin is)

Season the pumpkin lightly with salt. Spread the bread on both sides with butter or margarine. Reserve extra butter or margarine for dotting on top. Grease the base of a saucepan with butter or margarine. Layer the ingredients in the saucepan, starting with the bread layer, followed by a layer of pumpkin, then the sugar, cinnamon sticks and orange rind. Repeat the layers, ending with a pumpkin layer, and sprinkle sugar over. Dot with the reserved pieces of butter or margarine and cover with the lid. Cook over low heat until tender, or use an ovenproof glass dish and bake for 45 minutes at 180 °C. Add some water if the pumpkin becomes too dry. Serve hot.

VARIATION

Omit the sugar and spread apricot jam on the bread.

INA'S HINT: It's safer to bake the pumpkin in the oven, as it burns fairly easily in the saucepan on top of the stove. Cover the ovenproof dish with foil for the first 25 minutes, then remove the foil and bake until the pumpkin is cooked and browned. The apricot variation is really mouthwatering – don't be stingy; use a whole cup of apricot jam. This is delicious with fish braaied over the coals or an oven-roasted leg of lamb.

Mr Frederick Collair's first car and one of the first in Saldanha, a 1951 Austin A40. He was a fisherman from Saldanha and paid cash for the car.

'Pampoenmoes' (breaded pumpkin) is a delicious, old-fashioned accompaniment, usually served with a Sunday meal. Do not be tempted to stir the mixture.

Pampoenmoes

Orange sweet potatoes

6 SERVINGS

These are delicious served with fried fish.

4–6 medium sweet potatoes

SAUCE

2 c (500 ml) water
½ c (125 ml) freshly squeezed orange juice
½ c (125 ml) brown or yellow sugar
½ t (2,5 ml) salt
3 T (45 ml) golden syrup
grated rind of 1 orange
2 T (30 ml) butter or margarine

Boil the sweet potatoes, skin and all, in water until tender. Remove from the heat and drain. Peel off the skins, slice the sweet potatoes and pack in a medium-sized ovenproof dish. Heat the rest of the ingredients and stir constantly until the mixture boils. Pour the sauce over the sweet potato slices in the ovenproof dish and bake for about 35–40 minutes at 180 °C, until the sauce thickens.

Soetpatats

6 SERVINGS

Prepared correctly, 'soetpatats' (caramelized sweet potatoes) is a dish fit for a king!

4–6 medium sweet potatoes
2 T (30 ml) oil
1 c (250 ml) sugar
3 T (45 ml) butter or margarine
3 pieces stick cinnamon, broken into pieces
the dried or grated rind of 1 orange

Peel the sweet potatoes and cut them into slices. Heat the oil and ½ c (125 ml) sugar together in a saucepan until the sugar caramelizes and becomes syrupy. Layer the sweet potato slices and the rest of the sugar in the saucepan, ending with a layer of sugar. Dot pieces of butter or margarine, the stick cinnamon and orange rind on top. Reduce the heat, cover with a tight-fitting lid and simmer. Add a little water if the sweet potatoes are too dry. Serve with fried meat, or with custard, as a dessert.

Orange sweet potatoes

Sweetened barley

8 SERVINGS

Nothing could be more typical of West Coast fare than sweetened barley.

2 c (500 ml) barley
6 c (1,5 litres) water
½ t (2,5 ml) salt
2 pieces stick cinnamon
5 T (75 ml) sugar
3 T (45 ml) butter or margarine
⅓ c (80 ml) seedless raisins (optional)

Soak the barley overnight in 4 c (1 litre) water.

Drain, add 2 c (500 ml) water, salt and cinnamon and cook until the barley is tender, stirring from time to time. Add the sugar, butter or margarine and raisins (if using) and cook for a further 10 minutes over low heat. Stir constantly until the mixture looks like oats porridge, adding a little water if too thick. Serve with fried meat or fish.

Sweetened samp

6–8 SERVINGS

1 kg samp
8 c (2 litres) water
3–4 c (750 ml–1 litre) milk
2 t (10 ml) salt
3 pieces stick cinnamon
⅘ c (200 ml) sugar
⅖ c (100 ml) butter or margarine
½ c (125 ml) seedless raisins (optional)
2–3 T (30–45 ml) cornflour (if necessary)

Soak the samp overnight in 4 c (1 litre) cold water.

Drain the samp and cook in 4 c (1 litre) fresh water until tender. Drain, but reserve the cooking liquid. Place the cooked samp in a clean, heavy-based saucepan and add the rest of the ingredients (excluding the cornflour). Bring to boiling point, reduce the heat and cook until thickened, stirring from time to time. If the mixture is not thick enough, thicken with cornflour mixed with a little of the cooled cooking liquid. Serve as a side dish with a roast, stew or fried fish.

A tasty, old-fashioned fisherman's food for the winter months, when money is scarce. Sometimes it is even served as a dessert.

The harbour at Lambert's Bay.

Dessert remains everyone's favourite, especially if it's a pudding that recalls the happy memories of days spent with your grandmother in her kitchen. What could be more satisfying than something sweet to round off a hearty meal?

SWEET TRADITION

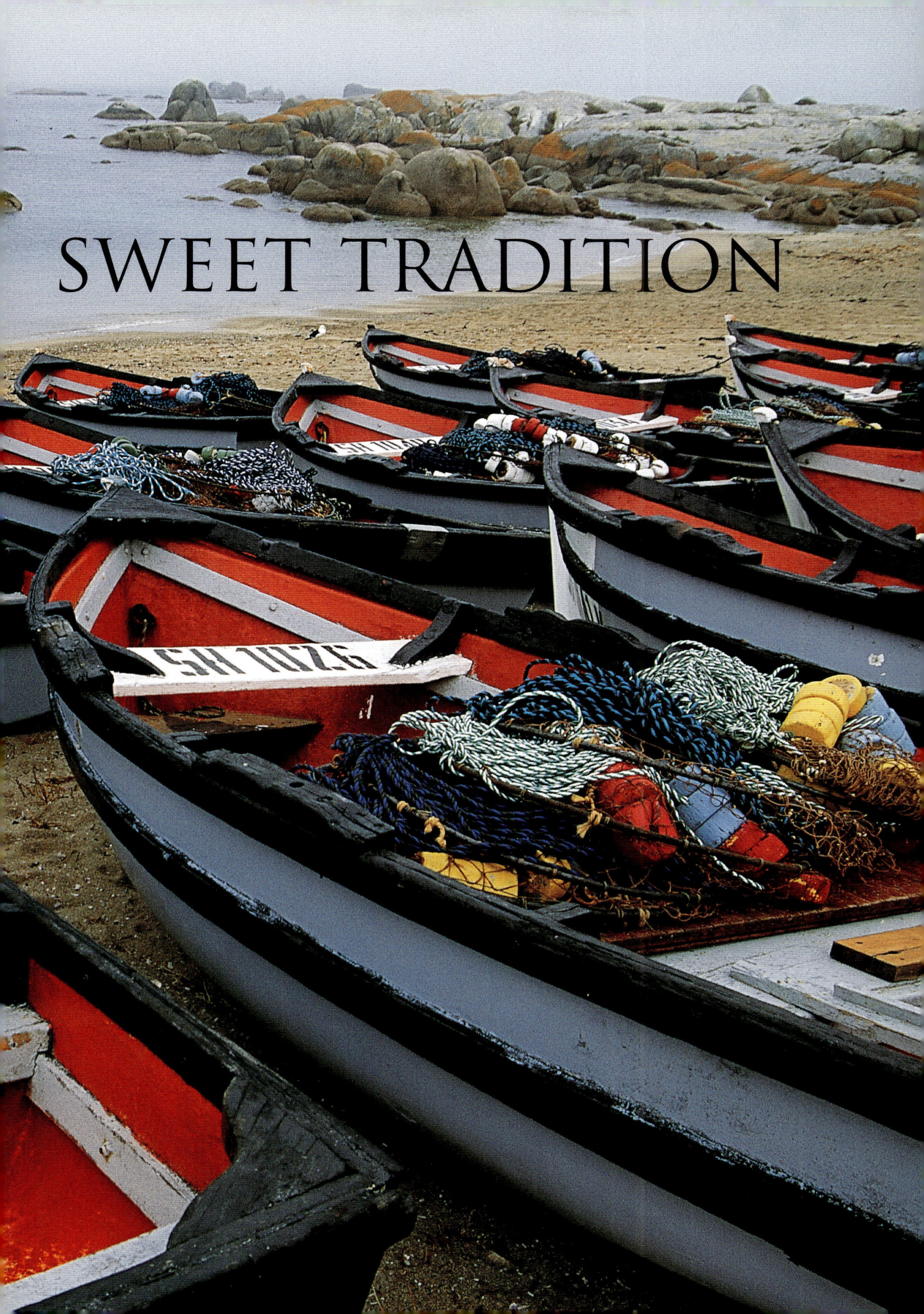

Apple crumble tart

6 SERVINGS

The crumble of this old-fashioned pudding is made with cornflakes and condensed milk.

4 large Granny Smith apples
2 whole cloves
2 c (500 ml) water
½ c (125 ml) desiccated coconut
½ c (125 ml) brown sugar
1½ c (375 ml) cornflakes
1 can (397 g) full-cream condensed milk

Preheat the oven to 180 °C.

Peel and slice the apples. Bring the apples, cloves and water to boiling point and cook until tender. Drain, remove the cloves and turn the stewed apples out into a greased baking dish. Mix the coconut, brown sugar, cornflakes and condensed milk together well and pour over the stewed apples. Bake for 30 minutes. Serve with custard or ice cream.

Economical souskluitjies

4 SERVINGS

3 c (750 ml) water
½ t (2,5 ml) salt

BATTER
1 c (250 ml) cake flour
2 t (10 ml) baking powder
½ t (2,5 ml) salt
1 T (15 ml) butter or margarine
1 egg, beaten
½ c (125 ml) milk

SAUCE
½ c (125 ml) sugar
1 t (5 ml) ground cinnamon
2 T (30 ml) butter or margarine

To make the batter, sift the flour, baking powder and salt together. Rub the butter or margarine into the flour until it looks like breadcrumbs. Mix the egg and milk together, and mix with the flour mixture to make a batter.

In a pot, heat the water and salt together to boiling point, then drop spoonfuls of batter into the rapidly boiling water. Cover with the lid and cook for 10 minutes; do not remove the lid. Spoon the dumplings into a heated serving dish and reserve the water.

Mix the sugar and cinnamon. To make a sauce, use the water in which the dumplings were cooked and mix with, a quarter of the cinnamon-sugar and the butter or margarine. Pour the sauce over the dumplings and sprinkle the rest of the cinnamon-sugar over. Serve with custard.

In the original 'souskluitjie' (cinnamon dumpling) recipe, our forefathers used water, not milk, in the batter because they could not always afford milk.

Economical souskluitjies

Jelly and custard pudding

8 SERVINGS

1 packet (40 g) jelly powder (strawberry, orange or lemon)
1 c (250 ml) boiling water
2 c (500 ml) full-cream milk
3 egg yolks
1 c (250 ml) sugar
3 egg whites, whisked until stiff

Dissolve the jelly powder in the boiling water. Leave to cool.

Heat the milk to just under boiling point and just before a skin forms on top. Beat the egg yolks and sugar together and add a little of the hot milk. Add to the saucepan containing the rest of the hot milk. Reduce the heat and stir constantly until the milk mixture thickens and coats the back of a spoon. Remove from the heat and stir the jelly mixture into the cooled custard. Allow to cool completely, until starting to set, then fold in the whisked egg whites. Turn out into a pudding dish and chill in the refrigerator until set. Serve with ice cream.

INA'S HINTS: Set the pudding in individual moulds or tea cups. Fill each to three-quarters full. Turn out onto large plates and decorate with fresh fruit in season. Sift icing sugar lightly over the plates.

To prevent the custard from curdling, beat 2 t (10 ml) cornflour into the egg yolk mixture.

Buttermilk pudding

6 SERVINGS

2 c (500 ml) buttermilk
2 c (500 ml) milk
3 eggs, beaten
1 c (250 ml) sugar
¾ c (190 ml) cake flour
6 T (90 ml) butter or margarine, cubed

Preheat the oven to 180 °C.

Mix all the ingredients together, excluding the butter or margarine. Turn into a large, greased ovenproof dish. Bake for 30 minutes, until set and golden brown. Place cubes of butter or margarine on top, and allow to melt into the pudding. Serve hot with custard.

Jelly and custard pudding served with a selection of berries

Quick brown pudding

6 SERVINGS

SYRUP
2½ c (625 ml) water
1 c (250 ml) sugar
1 t (5 ml) ground ginger
or 1 T (15 ml) grated fresh ginger

BATTER
125 g butter or margarine
½ c (125 ml) apricot jam
2 t (10 ml) bicarbonate of soda
½ c (125 ml) cake flour (unsifted)
a pinch of salt

For the syrup, heat the water, sugar and ginger in a saucepan. Stir until the sugar has dissolved, then heat to boiling point.

To make the batter, melt the butter or margarine and jam in another saucepan and add the bicarbonate of soda. Remove from the heat and add the flour and salt, then mix well. Drop spoonfuls of batter into the boiling syrup. Cover with the lid, reduce the heat and boil for 10 minutes. Do not remove the lid before the cooking time has elapsed. Serve with custard or cream.

VARIATION

Use cinnamon instead of ginger.

Orange pudding

6 SERVINGS

SYRUP
2 c (500 ml) freshly squeezed orange juice
½ c (125 ml) water
1 c (250 ml) sugar
2 T (30 ml) grated orange rind

BATTER
4 T (60 ml) butter or margarine
½ c (125 ml) milk
1 T (15 ml) grated orange rind
1 egg
1 c (250 ml) cake flour
a pinch of salt
2½ t (12,5 ml) baking powder
½ c (125 ml) sugar

Heat the syrup ingredients in a heavy-based saucepan. Stir until the sugar has dissolved, then heat to boiling point.

To make the batter, melt the butter or margarine in a separate saucepan, remove from the heat and beat in the milk, orange rind and egg. Sift the flour, salt and baking powder together into a mixing bowl and add the sugar. Add the milk mixture to the flour mixture and mix well. Drop spoonfuls of batter into the boiling syrup. Cover the saucepan with the lid, reduce the heat and boil for a further 15 minutes. Do not lift the lid before the cooking time has elapsed. Serve with custard or whipped cream.

Orange pudding with whipped cream

Old-fashioned bread pudding

8 SERVINGS

8 slices white bread, crusts removed
4 T (60 ml) butter or margarine
4 c (1 litre) milk
3 eggs
¾ c (190 ml) sugar
1 t (5 ml) vanilla essence
2 T (30 ml) apricot jam
1 t (5 ml) grated nutmeg

Preheat the oven to 180 °C.

Spread the bread with butter or margarine and arrange in a large ovenproof dish. Beat the milk, eggs, sugar and essence together well, then pour the mixture over the bread and dot with jam. Sprinkle nutmeg over. Set aside for 20–30 minutes, to allow the milk to be absorbed by the bread. Bake for 30 minutes in the oven, until the pudding has set and is golden brown. Serve with hot custard.

INA'S HINT: Spread butter or margarine and apricot jam on the bread – allow an extra ½ c (125 ml) jam for this.

Festive bread pudding with raisins

6 SERVINGS

This rich bread pudding is reserved only for special occasions.

1 can (410 g) evaporated milk
1 c (250 ml) water
4 eggs
⅓ c (80 ml) sugar
6 slices white bread
3 T (45 ml) butter or margarine
⅓ c (80 ml) apricot jam
4 T (60 ml) raisins

Preheat the oven to 180 °C.

Mix the evaporated milk, water, eggs and sugar together in a mixing bowl. Spread the bread on both sides with butter or margarine and jam and pack into a medium-sized, rectangular baking dish. Sprinkle the raisins over the bread, pour the milk mixture over and press down lightly with a fork. Set aside for 20 minutes. Bake for 30–45 minutes, until golden brown. Serve with hot custard.

Festive bread pudding with raisins

Peach dumplings

6 SERVINGS

SAUCE
250 g dried peaches
4 c (1 litre) water
4 T (60 ml) sugar

DUMPLINGS
¾ c (190 ml) cake flour
1 t (5 ml) baking powder
½ t (2,5 ml) salt
1 T (15 ml) butter or margarine
5 T (75 ml) boiling water
2 t (10 ml) cornflour
2 T (30 ml) water

Soak the peaches overnight in water. Heat the peaches and water in a large saucepan and stir in the sugar. Cook slowly over low heat until the peaches are tender.

Sift the flour, baking powder and salt together. Melt the butter or margarine in the boiling water and add to the dry ingredients. Mix to a stiff dough. Drop spoonfuls of dough into the peach sauce, cover and simmer until the dumplings are cooked. Spoon the dumplings and peaches into a serving dish, using a slotted spoon. Mix the cornflour with water and stir into the peach sauce. Boil until the sauce is clear and spoon over the dumplings and peaches in the serving dish. Serve hot with custard.

VARIATION
Make cinnamon-sugar by mixing 4 T (60 ml) sugar and ½ t (2,5 ml) ground cinnamon and sprinkle over the dumplings just before serving.

Sago pudding

8 SERVINGS

This ever-popular pudding is just right for a cold winter's day.

250 g sago
2 c (500 ml) hot water
4 c (1 litre) milk
½ t (2,5 ml) salt
3 pieces stick cinnamon
125 g butter or margarine, cubed
1 c (250 ml) apricot jam
4–5 extra-large eggs, beaten
1½ t (7,5 ml) vanilla essence

Soak the sago overnight in the hot water.

Preheat the oven to 180 °C. Heat the milk to just under boiling point and add the sago mixture, salt and stick cinnamon. Stir and cook the sago mixture until thick and transparent. Remove from the stove and cool slightly. Fold the butter or margarine and jam into the lukewarm sago mixture. Add the beaten eggs and vanilla essence. Remove the pieces of cinnamon and turn the mixture into a large, greased ovenproof dish. Bake for about 30 minutes, until the mixture is set and golden brown.

Sago pudding baked in individual ramekins

West Coast people are used to hardship. They know that food which may be plentiful today, could well be scarce tomorrow, so they have found a number of ways to preserve it, for the future when days are lean.

FOOD
FOR TOMORROW

Brawn

SERVES 8–10

Brawn is homemade cold meat. It is important to use the trotters as well, because they provide the natural gelatine that sets the brawn.

1 cow's foot or 4 sheep's trotters
500 g cow's or sheep's tripe
4 c (1 litre) water, or more if needed
½ c (125 ml) vinegar
salt to taste
10 whole cloves
1 bay or lemon leaf
10 peppercorns

Ask your butcher to clean the offal thoroughly.

Cook the offal slowly in the water in a heavy-based saucepan for at least 4 hours, until tender. Cool slightly, remove the bones and cut the meat into pieces. Return the meat to the saucepan, add the remaining ingredients and allow to cook well through. Remove from the stove, turn out into a shallow glass dish and leave to set.

INA'S HINT: To reduce the smell of the cooking offal, add an onion and a few slices of lemon to the meat in the saucepan while it is cooking.

Koep & Loep's own smoked mussels in oil

MAKES 10 KG

10 kg mussel meat
until very dry
sunflower oil
garlic flakes (optional)

Smoke the mussels in any small smoker until very dry. Pack the smoked mussels in jars. Pour over enough oil to fill the jars. As a variation, garlic flakes may be added. Close the lid tightly. The mussels will be ready to eat after a week. They are delicious on savoury biscuits or toast, with parsley and chopped sweet peppers.

Koep & Loep is the name of Umoya Fishing's fish shop in Sandy Point, St Helena Bay. A competition was held in 2001 to find a name for the shop. There were two strong contenders: Ocean Point (because the factory lies at the tip of the bay) and Koep & Loep (literally, buy and go). Eventually it was decided to combine the two names and the shop is now known as Ocean Point Koep & Loep.

Koep & Loep's own smoked mussels in oil

Ocean Point rollmops

MAKES ± 12 JARS

Barbara Brown's father was an expert rollmop maker, and he often prepared them for weddings. She learnt from him how to make the dish really special, and later developed her own variations.

10 kg fresh sardines, scaled and filleted
2,5 kg salt
32 c (8 litres) white vinegar
4 c (2 litres) water
1–2 whole cloves per bottle
10 chillies, finely sliced
6 large carrots, peeled and sliced
½ c (125 ml) peppercorns
2 cucumbers, sliced
12 bay leaves
red, green and yellow cocktail onions

Layer the fish fillets in a clean basin, right to the rim, salting each layer as you go. Cover and set aside in a cool place for about 5 days. Rinse the sardines thoroughly in water and drain. Mix the vinegar and water together, then add enough of the vinegar mixture to cover the sardines. Leave overnight. Drain. Roll the sardines up, skin side out, and secure with toothpicks.

Pour boiling water over the cloves, chillies, carrots, peppercorns and cucumbers to sterilize. Layer these ingredients, with the bay leaves, cocktail onions and rollmops in 400–500-g sterilized jars. Fill the jars with the vinegar mixture, cover with the lids and seal tightly. Store the jars in a cool place. Leave to stand for a minimum of 5 days before eating. Serve the rollmops with savoury biscuits.

Rollmops

MAKES 4–5 JARS

Sardines are the best fish for this recipe, although any oily fish, such as white stumpnose or yellowtail, may also be used. Delicious served with salad and bread on a hot summer's day.

1 kg fresh sardines
1 kg coarse salt
6 c (1,5 litres) white vinegar
2 c (500 ml) water
1 kg sugar
1 packet (40 g) pickling spices
oil

Remove the fish heads, squeeze out the entrails and fillet the fish. Do not remove the skin. Layer the fish and coarse salt in a basin and set aside overnight.

Rinse the fish fillets well and pat dry. Roll the fish up, skin side out, and secure with toothpicks. Heat the vinegar and water to boiling point, then add the sugar. Cook until the sugar has dissolved, then add the pickling spices. Cook for a further minute, remove from the heat and allow to cool.

Pack the rolled-up fish in 400–500-g sterilized glass jars. Fill the jars with the cooled vinegar mixture and add 1 T (15 ml) oil to each jar. Seal, making sure the jars are airtight. The rollmops will be ready to eat after about 3 days.

HINT

Store in the refrigerator – rollmops will keep for 3 months.

Rollmops

Dried snoek

4–8 SERVINGS

Snoek is salted and dried to preserve it for when this fish is out of season (during the warm summer months).

1 snoek
1 kg coarse salt

Remove the head and butterfly the snoek. Wash the fish and sprinkle thoroughly with coarse salt. Set aside for 3 hours, then rinse off all the salt. Hang the fish outside, in the sun, for about 7 days – weather permitting – until the snoek is completely dry. Snoek is dry when it has a golden-brown colour and the meat is firm and hard. Enjoy with fresh bread and jam.

HINT
Dried snoek may be cut into smaller pieces, brushed with oil, wrapped in waxed paper and stored in airtight containers. Alternatively, snoek may be cut up, wrapped in plastic and stored in the freezer.

Bokkoms

10 SERVINGS

On the West Coast, small harders (mullet) that are salted and sundried are called 'bokkoms' and are eaten as 'biltong' (dried meat).

1 kg coarse salt
4 c (1 litre) water
10 small harders

Make a pickling mixture (brine) from the salt and water. Place the fish in the brine and leave for 12 hours or longer, depending on the size of the fish. Rinse the fish well and, using a large blunt needle and string, thread the string through the fishes' eyes. Hang in the sun for 7 days, or longer, until the fish are hard and dry.

To serve the fish, remove the head and tail. Cut an incision along the backbone and remove the backbone. Cut open the stomach and remove the entrails, then pull the skin off completely. They are very tasty with fresh bread and apricot jam, and black coffee.

HINT
Bokkoms are not cooked – they are salted and dried. If they are too dry and hard, do what West Coast people do – heat bokkoms to lukewarm over the coals or in the oven, to make them softer and juicier.

Traditionally strung bokkoms drying in the sun

Snoekmootjie

5–6 SERVINGS

This is a good way to preserve snoek for when it is out of season. The fish will, in time, change colour; first to gold and then to brown. 'Snoekmootjie' (salted snoek portions) may be used for 'smoorvis' (braised fish) (see page 49). This is how Eric Wilsnach makes it.

1 whole snoek
2 kg coarse salt

Remove the snoek's head, but do not butterfly the fish. Cut out the fins on the back, and remove the entrails through an incision from the gills to the small ventral opening. Cut into 5–6 portions. Sprinkle 1 kg salt over the snoek, rubbing in well all over. Leave for 4 days, or longer, in an airtight container – a wooden barrel works particularly well. Rinse the snoek portions with brine. Return to the container and sprinkle another 1 kg coarse salt over. Seal and leave for 1 month or longer.

VARIATION

If the snoek is to be stored for longer than a year, add 1 packet (5 g) bay leaves and 1 packet (5 g) peppercorns, or 40 g pickling spices.

HINT

Reseal the container tightly after opening.

Green fig preserve

MAKES ± 10 JARS

The figs from the first crop of the season are used, while still hard, to make 'groenvyekonfyt' (green fig preserve).

2 kg green figs
20 c (5 litres) water
5 t (25 ml) slaked lime (from your chemist)
12 c (3 litres) boiling water

SYRUP

2,5 kg sugar
10 c (2,5 litres) water
2 t (10 ml) ground ginger
1 t (5 ml) lemon juice

Scrape the figs lightly with a fork, or grate the skin lightly. Rinse the figs and soak them overnight in a mixture of water and slaked lime. Rinse the figs and soak for a further 2 hours in fresh water, then add them to the boiling water and boil for 30 minutes, or until tender. Drain and cut crosses at the blossom end of each fig to ensure that the syrup (and not water) is absorbed.

Boil all the syrup ingredients together until slightly thickened. Add the figs, one by one, and boil for 1 hour, until the figs are tender and have absorbed the syrup. Pack the figs in warm, sterilized, 400–500-g jars, pour the remaining syrup over and seal.

Ripe fig preserve

MAKES ± 12 JARS

Throughout the year, glass jars of various sizes and shapes are cleaned after use and stored for making preserves. For this reason it is difficult to say exactly how many jars each batch of preserve will fill.

3 kg ripe figs
6 c (1,5 litres) boiling water
2 T (30 ml) lemon juice
1,5 kg sugar
2 t (10 ml) ground ginger

Scrape the figs and prick them lightly with a fork. Cut a cross in the blossom end of each fig. Place the figs in boiling water and cook for 10–12 minutes. Add the lemon juice, sugar and ginger and cook slowly, stirring constantly until the sugar has dissolved completely.

Reduce the heat and cook until the syrup thickens, constantly skimming off the scum that forms on the surface. Boil quickly for 15–20 minutes, until thick. Spoon into hot, sterilized, 400–500-g jars and seal immediately.

HINT

Preserves attain a lovely gloss if they're cooked rapidly.

Watermelon jam

MAKES ± 12 JARS

Homemade jams such as 'waatlemoenkonfyt' (watermelon jam) are much tastier than bought ones, and they cost less.

4 kg watermelon
3 kg sugar
juice of 2 large lemons
4 pieces dried ginger
½ t (2,5 ml) salt

Use the insides of a watermelon. Cube the soft watermelon flesh and remove all the pips. Heat the watermelon and sugar slowly to boiling point; stir constantly. Still stirring, cook slowly for 10–20 minutes until the sugar has dissolved. Add the lemon juice, ginger pieces and salt. Boil quickly, constantly skimming off the scum from the surface, until the jam is transparent and the syrup has thickened. Stir occasionally to prevent burning. Spoon the hot jam into clean, 400–500-g jars and seal.

HINT

Test the thickness of the syrup by dropping a little of the syrup on a saucer and placing it in the freezer. The syrup should be thick once it has cooled.

Ginger beer with a kick

MAKES 20 LITRES

In the past, ginger beer and 'dikkoek' (now known as 'plaatkoek' – two layers of a sponge cake sandwiched with icing) were all young people had for parties. They went on a picnic, or to dance in the bush, with a brown paper bag of 'soetkoekies' (traditional spicy biscuits) and a bottle of ginger beer.

500 g raisins, with seeds
1 packet (10 g) instant yeast
3 kg sugar
1 can (50 g) ground ginger
20 litres water

Rinse the raisins well. Place all the dry ingredients, including the raisins, in a large container (at least 25-litre capacity). Add the water, but do not stir. Close tightly and set aside for about 12 hours. Stir the mixture with a wooden spoon until all the sugar has dissolved. Cover and leave overnight, then pour the ginger beer through a muslin cloth and fill the bottles. Seal with corks, or cover with clingfilm. Leave to draw. The ginger beer will be ready after 2 days. Chill and serve ice-cold.

Pineapple beer

MAKES 22 LITRES

4 pineapples
3 kg sugar
1 packet (10 g) instant yeast
20 litres water

Remove the leaves and wash the pineapples well. Cut the whole fruit, peel and all, into pieces and place in a clean container with the sugar and yeast. Add water and cover. Leave to draw for 48 hours. Pour the beer through a muslin cloth, fill the bottles and seal. Chill and serve ice-cold.

Lemon syrup concentrate

MAKES 1 LITRE

2 c (500 ml) freshly squeezed lemon juice
1,6 kg sugar

Place the juice and sugar in a saucepan and heat slowly, over low heat, until the sugar has dissolved. The mixture must not be allowed to cook, otherwise it will become bitter. Set aside to cool down, then pour into bottles. Dilute to taste with cold water or soda water and serve ice-cold.

INA'S HINT: Lemons produce far more juice if they are left in hot water for 30 minutes before squeezing.

West Coast Idiom and Nicknames

Naive humour and a childlike sense of mischief were shared with delight and apparently helped the community to forget about its hardship. When he was a child, says Uncle Norman Wilsnach, entertainment was provided by catching snakes, collecting honey or sometimes simply by catching fish, tying their tails together with string and attaching tins to the string, then returning the fish to the water and watching them try to swim.

Unique expressions and even swear words, are characteristic of the idiom of West Coast fishing communities. The saying, 'hy vloek soos 'n matroos' (literally, he swears like a sailor [trooper]) is particularly appropriate here, and swearing is an integral part of their lives. It is also more prevalent among men than women. Coupled with this are pithy sayings that appear to be endemic to this particular region. Commonly used expressions and subtle extensions of meaning go hand in hand with life and work at sea, and some examples are sharply descriptive of the emotions and ideas of fishermen.

LAITSOG: When someone is not in a good mood, appears listless, or is annoyed and difficult, or simply bad luck. Laitchog, a variation, is used in St Helena Bay and along the Berg River

SOLDANA: Pronunciation of Saldanha in St Helena Bay and Velddrif

ONKEL: Uncle

STIEMMERSBAAI OR STIEMERS COVE: Steenberg's Cove – one of the historic towns on St Helena Bay

NOU BIETJIE DAG: Very recently

ONS HET GAAN WATERG HAAL BY DIE RISSIEWORGG: We went to collect water at the reservoir

DIE WATER GROEI OF VAL: The tide is rising or ebbing (literally, 'the water grows or falls')

VYFTANDVURK: To eat with the hands (literally, 'five-tine fork')

KOPPELOS: A fish line with two hooks and a fish attached to each, simultaneously

DIE WATER BRAND: When phosphorus reflects on the water (literally, 'the water is on fire')

DIE SKEI-RE LOOP: The boats come in, carrying fish

KOPMAN: Skipper

LIGMAAN: Full moon

PUSHED TO MOER: To be very tired; exhausted

TELLIE: You can go out again to catch fish – in the days before quotas

DIE WIND SKRAAL IN: The wind dies down and no longer blows so hard (literally, 'the wind gets thin')

DIE VIS LÊ ETTER-DIK: A dense school of fish

DIE VIS LÊ MODDERDIK: A school of fish, but not as dense as 'etter-dik'

DEKVRAG: The fish are not only in the hold, but also on the deck of the boat (literally, 'deck cargo')

HOLEVOL: The ship's hold is also full

DIE WATER IS TROEWEL: The sea is slightly rough

FRIES: Snoek, usually the largest, which are caught and taken home to be cooked or to give to someone. These days, they are sold

DOY: Sea gull catching fish

MY GELD IS GEGORREL AAN MY PENS: My money is tied around my stomach; usually on the way back from Walvis Bay after months away from home

KENTERWEER: The weather is going to change

BLÊNKSTIL: The sea is very still

DIE VIS RYS OP: The fish are rising, i.e. swimming very close to the surface

DIE VIS GEE OOR: When the weather is changing, the fishermen always think that they will catch a lot of fish (literally, the fish give up)

DIE WATER IS DOODSMOET: The water is very smooth and still

DIE WATER LYK SOOS 'N DAM: The water is very calm

DIE SEE IS PLANK: The sea is very smooth and still

GEE BOE-LYN: Pull in the (anchor) rope, it's time to go home as there is enough fish. The 'boe-lyn' or 'bo-lyn' is actually the mark on the upper line of a fishing net, which indicates whether the catch is poor (below the mark), sufficient or in excess (above the mark). The expression 'gee boe-lyn' is also used in the context of asking someone if you may enjoy a meal with them from the meat or other food they have in excess
DIS NOORD: Bad weather
HARRIG-VIS: Harders
KAP 'N STERN: Turn the boat
NET GEBOET: To repair the nets
DIE SEE JOPPEL: Small waves or ripples on the sea

The following nicknames are given to the people of West Coast towns, on the basis of the historical popularity of a certain seafood type or association:
MOSSELVRIETERS: The people of Paternoster (literally, 'mussel eaters')
BARVRIETERS: The people of Laaiplek and Velddrif (literally, 'barbel eaters')
HARRIRGS: The people of Langebaan (literally, 'harders' [mullet])
PATAT TRAPPERS: Less-than-flattering reference to the people of Hopefield (literally, 'sweet potato stampers or trampers')
DIE ELITES: The people of Saldanha Bay

Nicknames, familiar names and sobriquets are in common usage on the West Coast. They provide an insight into the language, culture and socio-political attitudes of its communities.

In certain instances, it is the norm to append a husband's name to that of his wife's. Apparently, there were originally only a limited number of names for women, therefore linking women to their husbands by name was a useful method of indicating relationship. Examples of this include Auntie Henna Kenna (Williams), Auntie Tos Victor (Basson), Auntie Cathariena Johnie (Williams) and Anita Klaas (Joshua). In similar vein, a mother's name would be added to that of her child, for instance, Klaas Koekie (Julies).

Other names are derived from physical appearance. Vettie (Dawid) Kleinsmith was stout; Jakob Horrelvoet (Andrew) has a clubfoot that causes discomfort when walking; 'Oom' Rooi Kallie (Wilsnach) had freckles and reddish hair; Longhie or Poy (William Joshua) was tall for his age in childhood. Later William became Willieboy or simply Poy. Pangha Vraagom was named after a fish and 'Oom' Bokkom Stringer was thin and, according to local opinion, a dry, sinewy-looking man. Because he is so thin, 'Oom' Andrew Carelse is teasingly nicknamed 'dolpen', a reference to the rowlock of a fishing boat, to which the rope of an oar is attached, while Dicky Kikke or Kakebeen refers to Dicky Engelbrecht, apparently noted for his characteristic jawbone.

The origin of some nicknames can be traced to the inability of children to pronounce a person's name correctly. Distortions such as Klongie, survived. Sometimes children were named after a grandparent or other family member and even inherited their nicknames. Aunt Tottie (Helena) Cloete was given her aunt's nickname, as well as that of her grandmother, Tossie. In St Helena Bay, four generations of Smith menfolk bear the nickname 'Hoender' (chicken). The source of some nick- or familiar names is totally unknown, even to their bearers.

Nicknames may be used to tease or in jest, or even to belittle the 'victim', but sobriquets are a sensitive issue, sometimes avoided entirely in the presence of the relevant person. Poverty and past embarrassments have also given rise to nicknames – subjects mostly avoided by older people. Racial issues in South Africa were reflected in names with reference to black, white and more derogatory titles, such as Wit Piet, Swart Willem, Kannetjiemeid and 'Oom' Kaffertjie, while diminutive forms are relatively common. By contrast, bravery resulted in a name such as 'Oom' Storm. He did not hesitate to go to sea in stormy weather.

The characteristic lifestyles of the people of the West Coast are illustrated in the variety of these forms of address. But it is preferable to hear them for oneself to truly appreciate the idiom, particularly when a delicious seafood potjie is bubbling over a crackling fire, or while a plump snoek is lovingly tended on the coals.

Recipe Index

PAGE NUMBERS IN **BOLD** TYPE INDICATE PHOTOGRAPHS.

Acknowledgements

This book represents the co-operative effort of a number of people. Every input, whether great or small, direct or indirect, contributed to the final result and thanks are due to all involved. *West Coast Cookbook* has initiated the preservation of the West Coast's heritage and it is hoped that others will be inspired to follow this example. However, a particular debt of gratitude is owed to the following people and institutions: Dr Neville Sweijd, former Deputy Director of the International Ocean Institute, Southern Africa, at the University of the Western Cape (UWC), and his successor Jocelyn Collins for their leadership; the Institute for Historical Research (UWC), which approached Dr Ernest Messina to write the historical background for the book; and Dr John van Diemel who recorded some of the interviews on videotape.

Without the immense contribution from the Canadian High Commission (Canada Fund) this project would not have been possible. Further contributions from Sea Harvest and the Saldanha Bay Canning Company are also appreciated. Diazville High School (Saldanha Bay) is sincerely thanked for the use of its facilities.

The people of the West Coast gave their time, shared their knowledge, opened their hearts and homes, and provided photographs, recipes and documentary sources. Special thanks are due to: Purie Africa, Ria Afrikaner, Judith Appels, Helen Arendse, Leen Arendse, Christine Arendz, Johnny Barends, Aunt Tos Basson, Hester Basson, Michael Beukes, 'Ouma' Lot Booys, Barbara Brown, Vera Bruinders, Aunt Lalie Cleophas, Aunt Tottie Cloete, Eunice Cloete, Norman Cloete, Aunt Baby Coetzee, Johanna Coetzee, 'Oom' Gollietjie Coetzee, Peter Constable, Joan Esau; Ellen Fester, Mr Goldsmith, Mrs Goldsmith, Alice Griffiths, Mrs Griffiths, Jocelyn Haricombe, Paul Haricombe, Dinah Jooste, Cynthia Joshua, William Joshua, Tom Julies, Aunt Suzie Julius, Fan Julius, Ellen Kotze, Helen Kotze, Hannes Lottering, Katrina Lottering, Mr MacLachlan, Mrs MacLachlan, 'Ouma' Anna Mitchell, Pauline Moses, Mrs Naidoo, Ocean Point Koep & Loep, Annie Orlam, Petronella Pharao, Sinie Pharao, Katie Prezens, Aunt Bawa Reid, Daphne Rossouw, Mrs Ruiters, Stephanus Ruiters, Nellie Samsodien, Leah Smeda, Marita Smith, 'Oom' April Snyders, Auntie Martha Solomon, Jane Solomons, Cecil Stoffberg, Cheryl Stoffberg, Myra Stoffberg, Bes Summers, Vanessa Summers, Caroline Talmakkies, Lenie Talmakkies, Charles Thomas, Mercia Thomas, Roy van Schalkwyk, Sanna van Wyk, Green Vigo, Anna Vraagom, Joan Vraagom, Lientjie Vraagom, Pangha Vraagom, Leslie Welman, Aunt Cathariena Williams, Caroline Williams, Henry Williams, Zelda Williams, Eric Wilsnach, Helen Wilsnach, Norman Wilsnach, Vernie Wilsnach.

Struik Publishers would like to thank the following for their significant contributions to the publication of this book: Ina Paarman; Dr Ernest Messina; Cynthia Joshua and Myra Stoffberg of the Bergrivier Visserssvroueverenniging; Sea Harvest, Saldanha; Lydia Britz from Sea Harvest, Cape Town; private fisherman Charlie van Blerk; and the Stofbergsfontein Homeowners Association. Thanks are also due to the following outlets for the loan of props: Antiques on Kloof, Gardens; @ Home, Cavendish Square; Bloch & Chisel, Diep River; Chinaworks, Harfield Village; The Cooks Room, Kalk Bay; House & Interiors, Claremont; L'Orangerie, Newlands and Wynberg Villages; Mad About House, Diep River; Moroccan Warehouse, Gardens; Ocean Basket, Gardens; and Plush Bazaar, Green Point.

Struik Publishers (a division of New Holland Publishing (South Africa) (Pty) Ltd)
Cornelis Struik House, 80 McKenzie Street, Cape Town 8001

www.struik.co.za

New Holland Publishing is a member of the Johnnic Publishing Group

Log on to our photographic website
www.imagesofafrica.co.za for an African experience

10 9 8 7 6 5 4 3 2 1

Translated from *Weskuskos* into English by Pat Barton

ISBN 1 86872 846 3

PUBLISHING MANAGER: Linda de Villiers
EDITOR: Cecilia Barfield
HISTORICAL CONSULTANT: Dr Ernest Messina
SENIOR DESIGNER: Petal Palmer
DESIGNER: Beverley Dodd
FOOD PHOTOGRAPHER: Neil Corder
STYLIST: Vo Pollard
FOOD PREPARATION: Reniet Geldenhuys
ILLUSTRATOR: Sean Robertson
PROOFREADER: Joy Clack
EDITORIAL ASSISTANT: Samantha Fick

REPRODUCTION: Hirt & Carter Cape (Pty) Ltd
PRINTING AND BINDING: Sing Cheong Printing Company Limited

PHOTOGRAPHIC CREDITS
Shaen Adey/Struik Image Library: pp 20–21, 28–29, 35, 69; Bergrivier Visserssvroueverenniging Beperk: pp 15, 18, 32, 56, 74, 80, 82, 94, 111, 112; Neil Corder/Struik Image Library: all food photography; Walter Knirr/Struik Image Library: pp 65, 86–87, 106–107; Ernest Messina: pp 7, 9, 14, 16, 17, 19; Cape Town Archives Repository: pp 4–5, 8, 10–11, 12, 13, 41, 66–67, 92–93, 97, 100, 102, 103, 130–131; Erhardt Thiel/Struik Image Library: pp 42, 85, 118–119, 137; Hein von Hörsten/Struik Image Library: p 117; Keith Young/Struik Image Library: pp 78–79.
The remaining personal photographs are the copyright of the individuals photographed.